JOE ORTON

Born in Leicester in 1933, Joe Orton gained entry to the Royal Academy of Dramatic Art (RADA) in 1951. By the time he left two years later, he was already living with his mentor and lover, Kenneth Halliwell. Orton did a brief spell as Assistant Stage Manager at Ipswich Rep in 1953 and worked part-time in a chocolate factory from 1957 to 1959, but mostly he and Halliwell lived on the dole – and wrote. Together they produced at least five novels, including *Lord Cucumber* and *The Boy Hairdresser*, between 1953 and 1960, by which time Orton had started writing on his own. First came the novel, *Between Us Girls*, followed by two plays, *Fred and Madge* and *The Visitors*, and a further novel, now called *Head to Toe*. Orton and Halliwell's only further artistic collaboration was the creative defacing of books from Islington Library, for which they served a six-month prison sentence in 1962.

After ten years of rejection slips, Orton finally achieved breakthrough in 1964 with the staging of *Entertaining Mr Sloane* and the radio broadcast of *The Ruffian on the Stair*. There followed in quick succession another stage play, *Loot*, premiered in 1965, and two television plays, *The Erpingham Camp*, screened in 1966, and *The Good and Faithful Servant* in April 1967. On August 9th that year, when he was due to meet the producer of a prospective Beatles film for which he had written the screenplay, Orton was found dead – murdered by Halliwell, who had then taken his own life.

Following Orton's death, *What the Butler Saw* was staged in 1969, his Beatles screenplay, *Up Against It*, was published in 1979 and the now famous *Orton Diaries* in 1986. John Lahr's biography, *Prick Up Your Ears*, subsequently filmed with a screenplay by Alan Bennett one of several volumes of published for the first time.

Also by Joe Orton

Autobiography
The Orton Diaries

Novels
Between Us Girls
The Boy Hairdresser *and* Lord Cucumber
Head to Toe

Plays
Fred & Madge *and* The Visitors
The Complete Plays

Screenplay
Up Against It

JOE ORTON

Fred and Madge

The Visitors

Two plays

Introduction by Francesca Coppa

NICK HERN BOOKS

LONDON

A Nick Hern Book

Fred and Madge and *The Visitors* first published
in Great Britain in 1998 by Nick Hern Books Limited,
14 Larden Road, London W3 7ST

Copyright © 1998 by the Estate of John Kingsley Orton
(deceased) professionally known as Joe Orton

Introduction © 1998 by Francesca Coppa

A CIP catalogue record for this book is available from the
British Library

ISBN 1 85459 354 4 (hardback)
ISBN 1 85459 359 5 (paperback)

Typeset by Country Setting, Woodchurch, Kent TN26 3TB

Printed by Biddles Ltd, Guildford and King's Lynn

Contents

Introduction

Joe Orton liked to give the impression that he had sprung, a
fully mature playwright, straight from the head of Dionysus.
For example, Orton claimed in *Plays and Players* that
Entertaining Mr Sloane, which won the London Critics' Award
for Best Play of 1964, was his first full-length play, and that
he had written nothing before going into prison in 1962 but
'a dialogue, set in a hospital, between a very old, dying man
and his 70-year-old daughter.' In point of fact, Orton's first
full-length play was *Fred and Madge,* written in 1959, and
the 'dialogue' he refers to was his 1961 play *The Visitors.*
Both plays are published for the first time in this volume,
and neither represents Orton's first literary effort.

Joe Orton actually began writing in 1953, a full ten years
before he became successful as a playwright. His career can,
in fact, be divided into three distinct phases, and the canonical
Orton works are products of the third phase, representing only
part of Orton's total literary output. In the earliest part of his
career, 1953 to 1956, Orton, under his birth name of John
Kingsley Orton, wrote as a junior partner in collaboration
with his lover Kenneth Halliwell. Together they produced at
least five novels, including *The Silver Bucket* (1953), *Lord
Cucumber* (1954), *The Mechanical Womb* (1955), *The Last
Days of Sodom* (1955), and the first of three works to be
entitled *The Boy Hairdresser* (1956). While these novels
attracted the attention of various publishers, they were all
ultimately rejected. In the latter part of 1956, Orton and
Halliwell decided to sever their literary partnership (although
they would reunite once more, in 1960, to produce the second
work called *The Boy Hairdresser*). From 1956 to 1962, John
Orton wrote as an independent author, producing two novels,
Between Us Girls (1957) and *The Vision of Gombold Proval*
(1961; published in 1971 as *Head to Toe*) and the two plays
in this collection. Orton's third play, also called *The Boy
Hairdresser,* was accepted by BBC Radio in 1963. Retitled

The Ruffian on the Stair, it marks the beginning of Joe Orton's mature career, which was cut tragically short when Halliwell murdered Orton, then killed himself in August 1967.

Joe Orton's mature work – seven plays, a risqué (and rejected) screenplay for the Beatles, and a literary diary unique in its combination of wit and sexual frankness – has had an enormous impact both on drama and on the culture at large. The plays have earned him a central place among 20th-century dramatists, and Orton's diary, which covers the last nine months of his life, is famous as a comic literary masterpiece, as a gay history, and as a socio-cultural record, chronicling Orton's vision of himself as a writer, as a homosexual man, and as a part of so-called 'Swinging London' during the so-called 'Summer of Love'. Furthermore, Orton's combination of subversive wit and pro-gay sensibility in the years before gay was good has earned him a kind of sainthood comparable to Oscar Wilde's among those interested in reconstructing gay culture and history. Most tellingly, the adjective 'Ortonesque' has firmly entered the lexicon as a precise way of describing a certain kind of provocative and outrageous comic vision.

Thirty years after his death, the publication of Joe Orton's surviving early works – *Lord Cucumber, Between Us Girls, Fred and Madge, The Boy Hairdresser,* and *The Visitors* – allows us to trace the development of Orton's extraordinary talent. Born to a working-class family in Leicester in 1933, John Kingsley Orton was an unlikely heir to Wilde, Austen and Congreve: he was a literary foundling if ever there was one. And yet, even Orton's very earliest writings – the juvenile diaries he kept between 1949 and 1951, between the ages of 16 and 18 – illustrate a determination, or even desperation, to make something of himself despite a lack of resources, encouragement, or support. It was this determination which kept Orton writing through ten long years of rejection, slowly developing the literary themes, techniques and style that would one day make him famous.

While Orton's adolescent diaries confirm his teachers' dismissive assessments of him – that he was semi-literate, that he couldn't spell – they also show his earliest attempts to self-educate and self-improve. Theatre was always Orton's chosen escape route. He joined a number of amateur dramatic societies, and his diaries record his desire to get parts, to improve his speaking voice, and to increase his grace and poise.

> 4 April 1949: Bought book its called *Look Your Best*. I wanted (for some hitherto undiscovered and probaly sentimental reason) *Richard III*, but couldn't get it. Found myself unconsciously think what I would say when asked to take part in a broadcast called 'How I became an actor' probably start, 'I think I have always had a sort of yearning etc etc' Pull myself together quickly.

Sixteen-year-old John Kingsley Orton saves money to buy books, theatre albums, and elocution lessons. Brought up in an anti-intellectual family and community, Orton nevertheless became a voracious reader, getting 'lots of books out of the Library' and using them to fill his many 'quiet' – which Orton always misspelt 'quite' – days. Orton's juvenile diaries also show him to be striving for personal and literary sophistication, and for wit:

> 24 February 1949: Our photos came today they are very good. Mam took them work the forewoman said she didn't know where we got our looks from as we didn't get it from mam. (Query: to believe or not to be, lieve.)

But Orton's quest for self-improvement was occurring in the vacuum of Leicester, and he was without the support of friends or family. It was none other than Laurence Olivier, via a newspaper article, who gave Orton hope that he might be able to attend RADA, the Royal Academy of Dramatic Art in London:

> 15 April 1950: Have been reading an article about the stage by Laurence Olivier. He says that there are scholarships one can win to the RADA. And for the exceptionally talented there are maintenance grants as well. Hope one of those elocution teachers I wrote to answers my letter. I should think one of them will. Failing this, I'll write to RADA itself. I know this address is GOWER ST – LONDON. But I must get an evenings job and how.

A line runs down the page from the word 'scholarships' to a plaintive note at the bottom – 'get it please'. Orton's desperation was fuelled by his hatred of the boring routines of menial work: his juvenile diary is a litany of complaints.

> 24 January 1949: Work, how I hate it in the morning when Dad says 'its 10 to seven' . . . .

> 27 January 1949: Not a very good day. Finished all my work so asked Horace he gave me some work. I didn't like cleaning ink wells.

> 21 April 1949: Mr Yates didn't come to work today so I had to help Becky (Miss Henry in Post room it was dead awful.)

But Orton's attempts to achieve something better were scoffed at by those around him: 'He came to me one day and said "I'm very interested in the theatre and the only thing I want to do is go on the stage",' remembered one of his teachers. 'I dismissed it.' But Orton stubbornly clung to his aspirations, seizing every opportunity to better himself and fighting tenaciously for small acting roles in local productions. On 17 June 1950, Orton recorded in his diary that he 'pulled an old dresser to pieces am trying to make a bookcase out of it if I can but there doesn't seem to be much good wood in it.' The future writer's rather poignant attempt to build a bookcase, in his world an uncommon and generally unnecessary piece of furniture, out of the meagre scrap materials then available to him, is symptomatic of the frustrations Orton faced in his struggle to become an artist and an intellectual, to become the kind of person who would want a bookcase in the first place.

Orton continued to work at jobs he hated in order to pay for elocution lessons: he wanted to improve the quality of his voice, and dampen the strong vowel sounds of his Leicester accent. The coaching apparently helped; Orton was accepted at RADA against considerable odds, and left Leicester for London in 1951. A month after the term started he stopped writing his juvenile diary, though not before he recorded having met Kenneth Halliwell, who was also enrolled in the acting classes. Once he became famous as a playwright, Orton tended to downplay his desire for an acting career. When his theatrical training later came up in press interviews, Orton tended to talk about his three-month postgraduate stint as an assistant stage-manager, emphasising its similarity to menial labour, and not about his histrionic ability or aspirations, or his love of the theatre as an adolescent. Acting, however, was Orton's primary focus in the late forties and early fifties – as indeed it was Halliwell's – and only after their acting careers fizzled out did they begin their productive literary partnership.

Kenneth Halliwell, Orton's partner and lover, was initially the more accomplished writer. Halliwell's first work, a play called *The Protagonist,* dates from 1949, and was written for the Carlton Players, the local dramatic society in Halliwell's home town of Bebington, a suburb of Liverpool. Written before Halliwell went to RADA, the play is in many ways immature; however, it provides suggestive clues about the character of its twenty-three-year-old author. It dramatises the life of the actor Edmund Kean, but Halliwell shapes the story so as to emphasise and celebrate Kean's social and sexual defiance.

Underneath *The Protagonist*'s surface level of biographical melodrama is a homosexual conflict disguised as a hetero-sexual one. In the play Kean is confronted with a threat that would have been very real to Halliwell as an active homo-sexual in Britain in the late 1940s: the choice of blackmail or ruin as a result of overstepping the bounds of socially acceptable sexual behaviour. Halliwell's Kean has an affair with a treacherous married woman, who turns his love letters over to her blackmailer husband. Faced with the threat of a lawsuit and public exposure of his adultery unless he pays, the iconoclastic Kean refuses to settle. 'Though I be legally forced to pay, yet I'll drag that strumpet through the courts. All England shall see where the right lies. Though the strict law may go against me.' Society cannot tolerate such honesty, and the great Edmund Kean is destroyed. But by having his protagonist refuse sexual shame and proudly proclaim what conventional morality demands he deny, Halliwell makes Kean into an early martyr of the sexual revolution in general and of gay liberation in particular; Halliwell's Kean 'comes out' as a sexual nonconformist, and his passionate arguments in favour of sexual freedom – codified and condensed – would be on pro-gay banners, buttons and bumper-stickers by the late sixties. Edmund Kean was Kenneth Halliwell's idea of a hero, and his creation in 1949 shows that Halliwell was socially, if not artistically, *avant-garde.*

The Protagonist thus gives us a rare, if sketchy, view of the young Kenneth Halliwell; it indicates that Halliwell was a romantic, that he was educated, that he endorsed moral and sexual defiance, and that he was ambitious. One can imagine how these qualities impressed John Kingsley Orton, who had only recently – and with great difficulty – escaped a life of harshness, deprivation and restriction. Up until recently, Orton had felt tethered to an abusive home and a menial job, and Halliwell, whose pose and prose were expansive, overblown, larger-than-life, must have staggered him. In light of the pathos of Halliwell's last years, it may be difficult to imagine him as a Byronic hero; yet that was certainly how he must have appeared to Orton in 1951. When Kenneth Halliwell abandoned acting for writing, John Kingsley Orton signed on as his apprentice. As the senior writer of the team, Halliwell dominated their early works; however, he also unselfishly and effectively nurtured Orton's talent.

Kenneth Halliwell was an ideal mentor for Orton because he possessed, as John Lahr aptly noted in *Prick Up Your Ears,* vocabulary, tenacity, and a sense of literary tradition. Halliwell, who was well and widely educated, was deeply interested in what, for lack of better words, we now might call the queer literary canon; he had distinguished a strain within the broader literary tradition with which he particularly identified, and to which he wished to contribute as a writer. Halliwell schooled Orton in these works, from the ancient Greeks to Christopher Marlowe to Jean Genet, and Orton came to share his literary tastes and perspective. Together they attempted to write works with a distinctively homosexual sensibility, and their early novels are all profoundly influenced by the style of Halliwell's literary idol, Ronald Firbank.

Firbank is the real godfather of gay literature, since he was the first author in the modern era to write queerly with a clear view of the potential consequences. Firbank was nine at the time of Wilde's trials in 1895, and they obsessed him throughout his life: he clearly understood the risks and ramifications of his own militant homosexuality. Nevertheless, Firbank was the first author to pick up the threads of aestheticism that had been dropped by Oscar Wilde, deliberately connecting himself to literature which was widely regarded as tainted, or even poisonous. In *Prancing Novelist: A Defence of Fiction in the form of a Critical Biography of Ronald Firbank,* Brigid Brophy notes that:

> Just as he put into modern practice Oscar Wilde's aesthetic theory, so Firbank modernised Oscar Wilde's camp. Firbank is perhaps the inventor, certainly the fixer, of modem camp. Popes, cardinals, choirboys, nuns, flagellants, queens (both senses): all the classic camp dramatis personae are his. He borrowed even Wilde's engaging camp habit of sending up the Queen (regnant sense.) Their queen – Wilde's and the one set firm in the imagination of Firbank, who was 15 when she died – was of course Queen Victoria.

'Sign your name Queen Victoria,' cajoles Inspector Truscott in Orton's *Loot,* 'no one would tamper with her account.' Firbank's classic camp cast of characters, sassed up for the sixties, reappear in Joe Orton's mature play as well as in some of the novels; in his adult diary, Orton refers to Firbank respectfully as 'the source'. It was Kenneth Halliwell who gave Orton his taste for Firbank, who outlined and then radicalised Orton's literary tradition. Firbank deeply admired Wilde, who had admired Jane Austen; Orton, trained by the Firbank-influenced Halliwell, was later pegged 'the Oscar Wilde of Welfare State Gentility', and was delighted when he was compared to Austen. It was the astute *Sunday Times* critic Harold Hobson who made the connection:

> I hope I shall not be misunderstood if I say that the English author of whom Joe Orton in *Entertaining Mr Sloane* reminds me most vividly is Jane Austen. Miss Austen had a keen eye for the absurdities of the fashionable fiction of her day; and so has Mr Orton. His *Entertaining Mr Sloane,* all proportions kept, is the *Northanger Abbey* of our contemporary stage.

'Hobson was the only critic who spotted what Sloane was,' Orton later admitted. 'This was absolutely amazing. I wrote him a letter saying that I've always admired Austen's juvenilia.'

Even after Orton became successful, Halliwell continued to
encourage his development, pushing him to broaden the scope
of his works, to expand his literary boundaries, to extend his
frame of reference. In his diary, Orton records how Halliwell
directed his literary career:

> I had the idea that the play I intend to write set in prison,
> *Where Love Lies Bleeding,* should be, in the main, a satire
> on Genet using much of the story of *Querelle of Brest.*
> K.H. said, 'You must use all Genet's subjects – beautiful
> young murderers, buggery, treachery, bent and brutal
> policemen and theft.'

And it was Halliwell, the former classics scholar, who pushed
Orton to connect his work back to the ancient Greeks, the
starting point of any gay male tradition. As Orton noted in his
diary:

> I've finished typing *What the Butler Saw* today. Yesterday
> Kenneth read the script and was enthusiastic – he made
> several important suggestions which I'm carrying out.
> He was impressed by the way in which, using the context
> of a farce, I'd managed to produce a *Golden Bough* sub-
> text – even (he pointed out) the castration of Sir Winston
> Churchill (the father-figure) and the descent of the god
> at the end – Sergeant Match, drugged and dressed in a
> woman's gown. It was only to be expected that Kenneth
> would get these references to classical literature. Whether
> anyone else will spot them is another matter. 'You must get
> a director who, while making it funny, brings out the
> subtext,' Kenneth said. He suggests that the dress Match
> wears should be something suggestive of leopard skin – this
> would make it funny when Nick wears it and get the right
> 'image' for the Euripidean ending when Match wears it.

On the surface, Orton is praising Halliwell for 'recognising'
his classical literary allusions; however, the parenthetical
'(he pointed out)' shows Orton admitting that something more
complex was happening. The passage – which is quite different
from Orton's normal way of discussing his writing – has the
tone of a student quickly reviewing notes given by an admired
teacher. Kenneth Halliwell was not simply 'getting' Orton's

themes, but discovering them, or even creating them, and by doing so, helping to knit Orton into the greater literary tradition.

Halliwell and Orton's early novels – *The Silver Bucket, Lord Cucumber, The Mechanical Womb, The Last Days of Sodom,* and the first version of *The Boy Hairdresser* – were all rejected by publishers, largely, if you read between the lines, on the grounds that they were too queer for mainstream audiences. In the days before the power of the pink pound was recognised, publishers thought that the homosexual audience was too small, and too marginalised to be addressed. However, the importance of these works in the development of the Orton style was critical. Imitating Firbank gave Orton not only a tone, but a methodology he would use throughout his career: collage.

Ronald Firbank was a literary mosaicist who wrote phrases on bits of paper which he eventually synthesised into a final product. Orton adopted a similar technique; he composed pages and pages of discrete phrases and fragments which he only later grouped into sentences, paragraphs, and pages. Orton wrote a novel's worth of words, just not in any particular order, compiling pages of unusual adjectives (affably, athletically, allergically, apocalyptically), prospective titles (*Under Mummy, Leave Her Alone, Phallic Necessity, Up the Nape, Hips and Whores, Queer Cactus, Emerald Has Been Stung by a Wasp),* and impressionistic Firbankian sentences:

> The sea was grey, marbled with glittering crests.
> Brown and silver gardens came down to the pink water.
> Pendant globes of orange and blue striped fruit.
> A picture of a gold woman with crimson eyes, wrapped
>   in fur.
> Windows like three orange eyes peering out of the fog.
> A sea like luminous milk.

Orton composed page after page of sentences like these, crossing them out as he placed them within a work. He continued to use this collage technique after he became a successful playwright; then, however, he compiled massive lists of more developed, distinctly 'Ortonesque' phrases which could be inserted into a play as necessary. These lists contain lines from Orton's major plays which, though conceived out of context, now seem intrinsic to the plays in which they were used; the unused ones also provide us with a glimpse at the plays Orton might later have written:

> – I doubt whether anything about a man's private parts would interest her. She treats them like bound volumes of Dickens. Peeping now and then when some musical tells her they're the 'in' thing.

> – Are you a good boy?
> – Yes.
> – Why are you wasting my time then?

> – Anyone over forty is led to believe that the younger generation are sexually insatiable. Isn't this true?
> – No, sir.
> – Another cherished belief exploded. The iconoclasm of today's youth is terrifying.

Orton also left us a list of appropriately 'Ortonesque' titles for these unwritten works. Orton used two of them – *Until She Screams* and *Up Against It* – before he died. We can only imagine the plays that would have been appended to some of the others: *Men and Boys; The Four-Letter Word Revue; Gwen, Maddened by Lust; By The Short Hairs.* One such title, suggested by Halliwell, was intended for Orton's next play, which was to be set at the coronation of Edward VII. Instead, John Lahr used it to title Orton's biography: *Prick Up Your Ears.*

After co-authoring their five failed Firbankian novels, Orton and Halliwell stopped collaborating. In a 1957 letter, Orton informed the publisher Charles Monteith of Faber and Faber that 'Kenneth and I have decided that there is very little to be gained by our collaboration and so we have split (for the purpose of writing).' By this time, Orton had already learned enough from Halliwell (and Firbank) to consider going out on his own; he had absorbed a literary tradition, adopted a non-naturalistic style, and developed a writing process which suited him. He had also mastered many of Halliwell's accomplishments: now Orton also had vocabulary, tenacity and a literary tradition. By fully utilising his two resources – Kenneth Halliwell and the public library – the determined Orton, like many autodidacts, had given himself a better education than most of the more fortunate get at school. Halliwell had shared his knowledge and skills with Orton, but it was Orton himself who was able to parlay those assets into a successful literary career.

No one can say with specificity or scientific precision why one writer fails while another succeeds. However, Orton's early solo work shows that he had one definite advantage over Kenneth Halliwell: he was interested in and paying attention to trends in contemporary writing. Orton and Halliwell began to write separately at some time in late 1956, a year which has come to be regarded as a watershed in British cultural history. Few contemporary British histories fail to note that 1956 was the year of John Osborne's *Look Back in Anger,* a play that was said to have triggered a dramatic revolution. Osborne and his semi-autobiographical protagonist, Jimmy Porter, were quickly described as 'angry young men', a label that connected them to fiction writers such as Kingsley Amis and John Wain, and to the young pop philosopher Colin Wilson, whose best-selling book *The Outsider* was published in the same month that *Look Back in Anger* premiered. Although these writers denied that they formed any sort of cohesive literary movement, the artistic press found the idea hard to resist, and hyped both 'angry literature' and 'the new drama', helping to create a market for both. As a result, novels featuring angry anti-heroes became popular in the late fifties, and a host of new playwrights, as diverse as Arnold Wesker, Robert Bolt, N.F. Simpson, and Harold Pinter, energised the theatre.

While Kenneth Halliwell continued to write in the style of Firbank, producing *Priapus in the Shrubbery* in 1959, John Orton experimented with the popular new styles and forms. In the second, more independent phase of his career, Orton wrote a diary novel (*Between Us Girls*), an 'angry' novel (*The Boy Hairdresser*), a Swiftian satiric fable (*The Vision of Gombold Proval*), and two startlingly different plays: *Fred and Madge,* and *The Visitors.* These works are striking in their diversity, and show Orton's desire to stretch himself, to learn to connect with an audience. He abandoned Halliwell's literary models, but not his values; rather, he must have realised that angry literature and the new drama had created a literary environment in which the kind of attack on bourgeois convention that Halliwell desired was not only acceptable but wildly applauded. As early as *The Protagonist,* Halliwell had argued that marriage was a locus for both economic and sexual oppression; this argument, heretical and obscure in 1949, with England anxious to return to normality after the war, had been used to great effect in *Look Back in Anger.* Anti-establishment literature had finally arrived, and Orton attempted to adapt his themes to its structures.

John Orton's dramatic writing would make him famous. In his first two plays, Orton explored many of the characters and themes which would mark his later, mature writing. Orton's first play, *Fred and Madge* (1959), fused anger and absurdism. Fred and Madge are a working-class couple who are trying to break out of the dehumanising routines of working-class life. However, those routines are partially represented by the rituals of theatre itself. *Fred and Madge*'s characters are aware that they are in a play, and one of Fred's menial jobs is to move the play's props and scenery (a job Orton, once an assistant stage manager, knew well). As the play progresses, the action becomes increasingly absurd, the language more fantastic and nonsensical. Fred, Madge and their friends escape from their constricted working-class lives into a poetic Firbankian fantasy, a progression that mirrors Orton's own escape from Leicester to literature.

At the beginning of *Fred and Madge,* Orton treats themes he would later rework in his brilliant (and underrated) 1964 play, *The Good and Faithful Servant. The Good and Faithful Servant* tells the story of George Buchanan, a man who has given fifty years of his life (and lost one of his arms) to his job at 'the firm'. He retires, old and broken, his faithful service rewarded with the firm's gifts of a broken toaster and a clock that runs backwards. Buchanan dies shortly thereafter, but not before he and his wife Edith have coerced their rebellious young grandson, Ray, into taking a conventional job and a wife, dooming him to repeat his grandfather's life.

Like Buchanan and Edith in *The Good and Faithful Servant,*
Fred and Madge have spent their lives proudly working at
brutal and pointless jobs, but Orton here plays the tune in
an absurd key: Fred rolls boulders up a ramp, and Madge
transports water in a sieve. Fred demonstrates his pride in this
good, honest work in a hilarious interview with a 'small part
player' (SPP):

SPP. You seem to have a really worthwhile job here.

FRED. We have our coats off, sir. Work is recognised as
   a virtue.

SPP. You push this stone –

FRED. Up the hill, sir.

SPP. And what happens then?

FRED. It all depends. It should roll down again. But
   accidents will happen. Sometimes it topples over the
   other side.

SPP. Tell me, what made you take up this work?

FRED. The security, sir. And I did want to be a useful
   member of society. I've worked here since I left school.
   Twenty-four years, I've worked at this job. Twenty-four
   years.

SPP. That's good to hear.

FRED. Almost half-way. In another twenty-six – not long
   is it, sir? – in twenty-six years I'll be able to retire. I'm
   making exciting plans for my retirement, sir.

SPP. It won't be long now.

FRED. It isn't long. Oh, the young people of today don't
   know what they're missing. They turn up their noses at
   jobs like this which offer security.

Bourgeois clichés – 'work is recognised as a virtue', the need
for 'security', being a 'useful member of society' – both entrap
and sustain Fred in his Sisyphean task; similarly, Madge and
her co-workers at the water-sieving plant break into virtual
choruses of proverbs:

QUEENIE. God's good.

MADGE. Look on the bright side.

GLADYS. Take the rough with the smooth.

QUEENIE. Into each life some rain must fall.

GLADYS. I couldn't bear to be in one of these dead-end
    jobs. I like to feel I'm doing something useful.

MADGE. I know what you mean.

GLADYS. I'm helping to make the world go round.

Through these dialogues, Orton argues that the exploitation of
the working class is greatly aided by this kind of thinking in
proverbs and clichés – the limitations of these characters' lives
are reflected in the limitations of their speech and their ideas.
Throughout his career, Orton would create humour from the
disjunction between what people say, who they are, and what
they do. Here in *Fred and Madge,* as in *The Good and Faithful
Servant,* the characters who have been most oppressed by the
class-system are those most deeply immersed in its rules and
values, and most brainwashed by its language.

However, unlike Buchanan in *The Good and Faithful Servant*,
who never realises the waste of his life until it is too late, Fred
finds himself increasingly dissatisfied with his life and decides
to leave both Madge and his job at the end of the play's first
act. The severing of the chains of marriage and work frees
Fred, but also allows Orton to shift the action away from the
kitchen sink and toward the fantastical. Orton once declared
that he was 'a great believer in the absolute logic of *Alice in
Wonderland',* and he gleefully allows that absurd logic to
govern the developing events of his first play. The second and
third acts of *Fred and Madge* are high-spirited, with Orton
clearly relishing the escalating nonsense. Madge's sister
Queenie marries an Indian and encourages all the women
to enter his harem. Fred and Madge, in a parody of Noël
Coward's *Private Lives,* meet in the hospital after both having
had accidents during their simultaneous second weddings.
Madge reschedules her wedding and invites two professional
insulters – or rather, an insulter and an 'insultrix', Dr Petrie and

Grace Oldbourne – to attack the guests. Wedding presents –
including an Oedipus complex, an old wife's tail, grandstand
tickets for the rat race and a pair of glasses for seeing the
better side of people – start rolling in. The characters, as a
party game, decide to 'have a go' at Modern Youth; Orton
gleefully organises them into a chorus of conservative
complainers and gives them a suggestive refrain, 'Oh there's
something queer about Brian.' Fred's father, a gardener like
Orton's father, suddenly and inexplicably finds he has green
fingers – plants start growing like mad, and England begins to
return to a green wilderness. Fred organises an expedition to
destroy British architecture by laughing at it: the buildings
literally crumble under this assault. By the end of *Fred and
Madge*, the combination of insults and laughter have resulted
in the liberation of the working classes and the destruction of
England. 'Do you want to ruin society and civilisation with
your laughter?' asks a reproving character. 'Yes, oh yes,'
exclaims Madge.

As England reverts to a primeval forest, the group decides to
emigrate to India; not the colonial India, but a fantasy India,
in fact a Firbankian India:

> FRED. We shall be the favourites of princes; ride in
>   howdahs and palanquins; live in purple-hued throne
>   rooms; dine off golden platters; listen to the music of
>   flutes; watch the dancing of exotic slaves –
>
> PETRIE. – of either gender.
>
> MADGE. How marvellous!

Fred and Madge's characters reject the English for the exotic,
while Orton explodes his characters' proverbial speech patterns
and substitutes the baroque, Firbankian lavishness that he
loved. 'The swaying palms and the camels and the seductive
dances of the Murri-murri, oh I can see it all,' exclaims Fred,
glorying in his new vocabulary. The characters bid farewell to
the audience and leave the play for the promise of an unlikely
Firbankian utopia, but as Dr Petrie spells out for the audience,
'We shall not despise the unlikely.' In the final lines, Orton
explains the philosophy of his play (and justifies its flaws)

by having Dr Petrie assert the importance of 'the improbable, the incredible, and the contrary to reason.'

Orton's next play, *The Visitors* (1962), was favourably regarded by both the Royal Court and the BBC, though both ultimately rejected it. The play tells the story of Mrs Platt's visit to her dying father in hospital, and shows Orton attempting a more straightforward illustration of his mastery of working-class idiom: both the Royal Court and the BBC thought the dialogue 'excellent', but rejected the play on structural grounds. Kemp, the dying father, is forced to listen to the relentless and false cheeriness of his daughter, who, like Madge and her friends in *Fred and Madge,* speaks in platitudes, generalities, and clichés:

MRS P. You've got years ahead of you.

KEMP. They'll have to carry me out.

MRS P. You mustn't say that.

KEMP. I shall be here until they carry me out.

MRS P. We'll have you skipping about in no time!

KEMP. I won't bother you much longer.

MRS P. I won't have that kind of talk, do you hear? You've years ahead of you. What do you want to die for?

KEMP. I don't want to.

MRS P. Well?

KEMP. But I'm going to.

MRS P. You'll outlive us all! People live to a hundred every day. You'll feel better once the fine weather comes.

Mrs Platt, in fact, appears to be Madge's sister, and in her flow of gossip she mentions many of the characters of *Fred and Madge,* while referring to different events: in *The Visitors,* Orton apparently decided to flesh out the same characters in a more naturalistic way. Orton repeatedly and obsessively rewrites his own work: in fact, Mrs Platt and Kemp are themselves the first drafts of the daughter and father duo, Kath and Kemp, in *Entertaining Mr Sloane.*

Like Kath, Mrs Platt is both infantile and infantilising ('Have a grape? Grapie? A little one?' she coaxes her father), and through a stultifying combination of childish optimism and fatuous propriety she prevents discussion of almost everything that Orton thinks important. Like Kath, and like the character of Susan Hope from Orton's novel *Between Us Girls,* Mrs Platt censors unpleasant language in herself and others, and the thoughts and ideas that such language expresses. In Orton's work, women are generally made to represent the false social niceties that prevent realities – work, sex, death – from being articulated and understood. The keynote of Mrs Platt's personality is represented by such censorious lines as: 'You're not to talk like that!', 'I won't have that kind of talk!', 'You can stop *dwelling* on that subject.' The fact that Kemp is actually about to die cannot be acknowledged in public, either by Mrs Platt or by the nurses who attend Kemp, although they admit as much back in the safety of the nurses' room. This cheerful misinformation understandably unnerves the dying man:

> KEMP. I've got no confidence in them. None at all.
> I wonder sometimes if we're safe in the hands of
> these nurses. Look at old Wilkins – talking about
> getting up on Friday. (*Pause.*) Saturday he was dead.

Kemp here is made to voice Orton's deep distrust of false language and prefabricated sentiment. Throughout his career, Orton unfairly associated this cheerful phoniness with women, ignoring their own oppression and focusing only on their role as oppressors. Lines such as 'As long as you keep cheerful, you'll be right as rain,' mark the nurses, with their controlling authority over Kemp and the other, male, patients on the ward, as the literary precursors of other female Orton characters. Orton would create another nurse in *Loot:* Fay, a woman who worries about keeping up appearances but 'has practised her own form of genocide for a decade'. Other Orton women are nurses in practice if not by profession. Tessa in *Funeral Games* cares for an an elderly man with a patronising and useless kindness ('Hum to yourself if you're sad,' she advises). Mrs Vealfoy, the corporate personnel manager in *The Good and Faithful Servant,* runs a social club for the elderly retirees of her firm, and prompts these old, exhausted souls to 'run through all the songs with "Happy" in them' – as if that could possibly compensate for a lifetime of labour and suffering. By *What the Butler Saw,* Orton was taking active revenge against the medical profession, and he happily has Mrs Prentice, who functions as the nurse of the Prentice sanitorium, beaten and put into a straitjacket.

Through these first two plays, Orton developed his female and older male characters. But it would be Orton's young men who would finally bring him success. Orton had created sexy young male characters in his novels, but he had yet to import them into his dramatic work. In his next play, *The Boy Hairdresser* (1963), he did just that; and the appearance of the young hooligan Wilson de-stabilises the duo of Joyce and Mike, producing a complex, dramatic triangle. Each of Orton's mature plays features a similar young delinquent: Sloane in *Entertaining Mr Sloane,* Hal and Dennis in *Loot,* Ray in *The Good and Faithful Servant,* Caulfield in *Funeral Games,* and Nick in *What the Butler Saw.*

The Boy Hairdresser was sold to BBC Radio in 1963, although Orton was asked to do rewrites. Between his play's acceptance and its broadcast, Orton revised both the play and his own persona. *The Boy Hairdresser* became *The Ruffian on the Stair,* and John Kingsley Orton, writer of ten years' experience, became Joe Orton, overnight success.

FRANCESCA COPPA

Francesca Coppa is Assistant Professor of English at Muhlenberg College, where she specialises in British drama and cultural studies. She has published and lectured widely on Orton both in Britain and the United States.

Joe Orton: a Chronology

1933   *1 January:* John Kingsley Orton born in Leicester
1944   Orton fails his eleven-plus exam
1945-47 Orton attends Clark's College
1949   Orton begins writing his juvenile diary
1950   *April:* Orton takes elocution lessons
          November: Orton applies to the Royal Academy of
          Dramatic Art (RADA) in London
1951   *May:* Orton starts at RADA
          June: Orton moves in with Kenneth Halliwell at
          161 West End Lane, London
          June: Orton stops writing juvenile diary
1953   *April:* Orton and Halliwell graduate from RADA
          April–July: Orton works as assistant stage manager at
          Ipswich Rep in Suffolk
          Halliwell and Orton begin collaborating on novels
          Halliwell and Orton write *The Silver Bucket* (novel,
          now lost)
1954   Halliwell and Orton write *Lord Cucumber* (novel)
1955   Halliwell and Orton write *The Mechanical Womb*
          (novel, now lost)
          Halliwell and Orton write *The Last Days of Sodom*
          (novel, now lost)
1956   Halliwell and Orton write *The Boy Hairdresser*
          (a novel in verse, now lost)
1957   *June:* Orton announces in a letter to the publisher
          Charles Monteith that he and Kenneth Halliwell have
          begun to write separately
          Orton writes *Between Us Girls* (novel)
1959   Orton and Halliwell move to 25 Noel Road, Islington
          Orton writes *Fred and Madge* (play)
          Kenneth Halliwell writes *Priapus in the Shrubbery*
          (novel, now lost). Orton and Halliwell begin stealing
          and 'creatively re-arranging' the jackets of books
          borrowed from the Islington Library

1960   Orton and Halliwell write *The Boy Hairdresser* (novel)

1961   Orton writes *The Vision of Gombold Proval* (novel, published 1971 as *Head to Toe*)

Orton writes *The Visitors* (play)

1962   *April:* Orton and Halliwell arrested for stealing and defacing library books

May–September: Orton gaoled at H.M. Prison Eastchurch, in Kent, and Halliwell gaoled at H.M. Prison Ford, in Sussex, for stealing and defacing library books

1963   Orton writes *The Boy Hairdresser* (play); revised title: *The Ruffian on the Stair*

Orton writes *Entertaining Mr Sloane*

August: BBC Third Programme accepts *The Boy Hairdresser* (*Ruffian on the Stair*)

1964   John Kingsley Orton becomes Joe Orton

6 May: Entertaining Mr Sloane produced at Arts Theatre Club, London

June: Orton writes *The Good and Faithful Servant*

29 June: Entertaining Mr Sloane transfers to Wyndham's Theatre

31 August: The Ruffian on the Stair broadcast on the BBC Third Programme

1964-66 Orton writes *Loot*

1965   Orton writes *The Erpingham Camp*

February: first (failed) production of *Loot*

1966   Orton writes *Funeral Games*

September: second (successful) production of *Loot*

*December***:** Orton begins writing mature *Diaries*

1967   *11 January*: *Loot* wins *Evening Standard* Award for Best Play of 1966. On the same day, Orton receives a letter informing him that *Loot* has also won the *Plays and Players* Award for Best Play of 1966

Orton writes *What the Butler Saw*

Orton writes *Up Against It* (Beatles screenplay)

June: under the title *Crimes of Passion*, Orton's one-act plays *The Ruffian on the Stair* and *The Erpingham Camp* are produced at the Royal Court Theatre

9 August: Orton murdered by Kenneth Halliwell, who then commits suicide

FRED AND MADGE

Characters

FRED
MADGE
QUEENIE
GLADYS
WEBBER
DR PETRIE
MISS OLDBOURNE
OLD MAN
SYKES
SMALL PART PLAYER

ACT ONE

Curtain up. Two fireside chairs and a standard lamp are visible. Silence. FRED *and* MADGE *are sitting, staring into the distance.*

FRED. Speak to me.

MADGE (*firmly*). No.

Silence.

FRED (*exploding*). Oh, the boredom! the fatigue of living! No merriment, no whoopie, no frolics. We never have a spree. Time hangs heavily on our hands. (*Pause.*) If we were animal lovers it would give us an interest in life. (*Pause.*) You do nothing to break the monotony. You haven't bothered. You've let things slide.

MADGE. I have the shoes to think about; the heels, the soles, the polish, the nails.

FRED. Shoes.

MADGE. – shoes!

Silence.

FRED. We could keep pets. (*Pause.*) What do you say to bats?

MADGE. What about the coal? They're heavy on coal. And coal isn't what it used to be. (*Pause.*) When I remember what it used to be like. The flames –

FRED. – how bright they were.

MADGE. How they leapt up the chimney.

FRED. Up and up, up and up.

MADGE. We couldn't look at the fire –

FRED. – keep away, you'd say, it's so bright!

MADGE. How bright it used to be.

FRED. And the nuts we roasted. All those nuts roasting in the flames. All those onions and potatoes in their jackets. Oh!

MADGE (*wistfully*). We've had some exciting moments.

FRED. – those onions in the winter –

MADGE. And there! think of the winter. It's all right in the summer, but in the winter you'll wish we'd never bothered. Bats are no company; they hibernate.

FRED. You're a hard woman.

Silence.

MADGE. What about the time you tried to breed locusts?

FRED (*in great agitation*). You make me lose confidence bringing that up.

Silence.

FRED. Do you think Queenie could lend a hand?

MADGE. I don't know; she has a lot on her –

FRED. – plate.

MADGE. A lot on her plate –

FRED. – plate.

MADGE. – running the snack counter. (*Pause.*) They do cold milk now as well as hot.

FRED. It's a dreary life.

MADGE. Where does it all lead?

FRED. Work, work, work, for forty years and all you get at the end of it is a pension. Not even a thank you.

MADGE. It isn't good enough.

FRED. People don't know how to treat one another.

MADGE. It's a shame.

FRED. Think of the things that could be done to improve

people's lives; they could do a lot to make things pleasant. They might have cards printed saying charming, delightful, felicitous things, and they could distribute them. Give people refreshing smiles in the street. Oh, there's a lot to be done. (*Pause. Bitterly.*) Not even a thank you!

MADGE. They don't stand up in the buses.

FRED. They don't raise their hats to a lady. Times are bad. Never raising a hat.

MADGE. – hats.

FRED. – hats.

MADGE. – nobody wears hats now.

FRED. Oh! I think the whole world has gone mad!

Silence.

MADGE. That's what it is.

FRED. Mad.

MADGE. You were always very perceptive, dear.

FRED. Mad.

MADGE. – put your finger right on the –

FRED. Mad.

MADGE. – heart of the matter –

FRED. Mad.

MADGE. – solve all our problems if we –

FRED. Mad.

MADGE. – did away with them all together. (*Pause.*) I'm frightened. I am. (*In a panic.*) I'm easily worried and depressed. Everything gets on my nerves. What's the matter with me?

Silence.

FRED (*in a low voice*). Bats.

MADGE. We've Janice to consider; she's a growing girl.

FRED. Bats.

MADGE. She's growing.

FRED. Growing all the time.

MADGE. It wouldn't be right for her sake.

FRED. No, it wouldn't be right as she's growing. (*Pause.*)
Think of a growing girl!

MADGE. She's getting big now. She's shooting up.

FRED. The expense is crippling.

MADGE. Yes, the expense is crippling.

FRED. I don't know which way to turn.

MADGE. It won't always be the same.

FRED. She'll stop one day.

MADGE (*brightly*). It's something to look forward to.

Silence.

FRED (*shocked*). She'll be gone from us. Gone! Our baby.
What will we do? What will we do?

MADGE. We'll be old.

FRED (*the idea sinking in*). Old. That's it! We'll be old. Every
minute we're growing older and older and older and older –

MADGE (*sharply*). Stop it!

FRED. – and older and older and older. Gradually mouldering
away. Turning to –

MADGE. Stop it, will you!

FRED. – dust. Turning to dust. Look at my hand, my arm;
they're firm now, they're young; in a few years I'll be
wrinkled, toothless, a mass of decay.

MADGE. Stop it!

FRED. I'll be bald. I'll be impotent. I'll be unable to climb
stairs. I'll be cold in the middle of summer. I'll be garru-
lous. I'll be drawing the pension. And soon after that –

MADGE (*hysterically*). Stop it! stop it! I can't stand it!

FRED. I'll be dead. What am I doing sitting here talking when I'll be dead? What am I doing, mouldering slowly into deaf and lonely old age? There's something wrong somewhere.

MADGE. What's it all for? (*Pause.*) I'm so depressed. My nerves are on edge. I think I ought to see someone about it. I ought to see –

FRED. You ought to see a doctor.

MADGE. I don't have faith in doctors.

FRED. No, you don't. And you need faith.

MADGE. And I don't have any. It's no good. No good. Everything looks black. What future have we? We've no future.

FRED. Age, aches, and the grave; that's the future.

MADGE. No future.

FRED. You've no faith. No faith.

MADGE. None at all.

FRED. Think of the times we could have had. The wasted opportunities. (*Pause. With inspiration.*) I could have been a clergyman; think of that!

MADGE. It's a good job.

FRED. Good wages and short hours.

MADGE. It's steady.

FRED. It's always there.

MADGE. It's stimulating. (*Pause.*) It's stimulating.

FRED. You give a lot of pleasure to others.

MADGE. It helps to make the world go round.

FRED. All the sermons I could have preached! All the marriages solemnised. (*Pause.*) I might have got my name in the papers! (*Pause.*)

Or I might even have been a bus conductor.

MADGE. There's a lot of climbing stairs on the double-deckers. (*In anguish*.) What if you were on a single-decker? Oh!

FRED. All the tickets I could have punched.

MADGE. Oh!

FRED. I can't bear it.

MADGE. I can't bear it. If you were on a single-decker and they made you climb the stairs – the danger!

FRED. The times I could have rung the bell and made out my returns and done overtime. Pounds out of pocket I am.

MADGE. So dangerous! I'd be a widow. Think of Janice and me left alone. Don't do it, for our sakes.

FRED. You're taken care of; I'm insured.

MADGE. What am I going to tell Janice? – she thinks the world of you,

FRED (*harassed*). I don't know what to do for the best. I'm out of pocket, and you worrying me – You'll have me in my grave. Here! see these? Grey hairs. Grey hairs!

MADGE. – oh, dear!

FRED. Grey hairs. I'm only thirty-nine. Thirty-nine; with more grey hairs than my father had when we buried him. He was eighty and not a grey hair.

MADGE. Perhaps it was dye.

FRED. Not a grey hair.

MADGE. Perhaps it was dye,

FRED. I'm going to pieces. This rushing about. Hurrying backwards and forwards. It's driving me out of my mind. (*Pause. In a panic.*) Do you know, this morning I – I forgot where I was going. I didn't know where I was going.

MADGE. You worry too much.

FRED. I worry over you and Janice and the house.

MADGE. Tossing and turning in your sleep. Worry, worry, worry.

Silence.

FRED. I forgot where I was going.

MADGE. Where were you coming from; that's more to the point?

FRED. I don't know.

MADGE. You don't know?

FRED. No.

MADGE. You don't know where you were coming from either?

FRED. No.

MADGE. It's very worrying.

Silence.

FRED. I found myself – there – in the street – wondering. I tell you straight, I'm all on edge. It's the life we lead. This coming and going, and the things they put in the bread.

MADGE. Chemicals.

FRED. The chemicals they put in the bread. It's not right. It's not natural. They should leave it alone. Leave it alone and we'd be all right. (*Pause.*) Oh, I get such a funny feeling sometimes.

MADGE. Funny feeling?

FRED. Here. In my head. As though I were going to do something violent.

MADGE. Something violent.

FRED. Yes.

Silence.

MADGE (*plaintively*). You never told me this before.

FRED. No.

MADGE. Why not? I have a right to know. I'm your wife.
And – Fred – listen to me.

FRED. I am listening.

MADGE. If –

FRED. I am listening.

MADGE. Yes.

FRED. I think I'd like to do something violent to you.

MADGE. Oh, dear.

FRED. – and to Janice.

MADGE. To Janice?

FRED. Do you both a mischief.

MADGE (*indignant*). Our baby? How could you. The times
you've told me what a blessing she is. The pleasure she's
given you. (*Pause.*) She's such a pet. Such a nice girl. She is.

Silence.

And she's popular. She must be the most popular girl in the
whole school. And it's frightened her. She isn't used to it.
It's had a peculiar effect on her; she's been off her food.

*Silence. He stares into the distance; his face wears a blank
look.*

She's on about learning to scrub floors; to scrub and polish
and cook – it's a job with a future. (*Pause.*) Can we afford
to have her trained, do you think?

Silence.

There's a lot of advantages. She'll be a goldmine; a classic
in her own right. If that's the career she's set on, then who
are we to stand in the way?

Silence.

FRED (*wearily*). It's time to change.

MADGE. A change is as good as a rest.

FRED. Time to go out into the streets; into the cold; into the harsh light. You'd better wrap yourself up.

MADGE. The weather's bad.

FRED. It might be raining.

MADGE. Clear the chairs –

FRED. – and the lamp.

MADGE. It's bitter out. I can't stand the cold. I'm not strong, not strong at all.

Enter QUEENIE.

QUEENIE. I've arrived.

MADGE. Hallo.

FRED *has wheeled a large bath forward.*

QUEENIE. What's the matter with him?

MADGE (*under her breath*). Take no notice, he's being awkward. (*Louder.*) I suppose you think that's funny?

FRED. What?

MADGE. You know very well. Don't you?

FRED. No.

MADGE. There's no need to show off because Queenie's here. A lamp-post is all we need. You can put that back where you found it and behave yourself.

He pushes the bath away.

QUEENIE. Sorry if I barged in. See you in a bit, then?

Exit.

Silence.

FRED *brings on a lamp-post and sets it up.* MADGE *changes her slippers for walking shoes and puts on her coat.*

MADGE. When are you going to stop making a show of yourself? Every time she comes you play up.

FRED. I don't know what we have to have her here for in the
first place.

MADGE. She's my sister.

FRED. Every night it's the same. She always chooses to come
when we're up to our necks changing.

MADGE. She can't help it.

FRED. She might give us a miss one night.

MADGE. It isn't her fault.

FRED. When you two have finished out here, don't expect
me to strain myself shifting lamp-posts backwards and
forwards. I'm fed up. See? Fed up. And I don't mean
maybe. Backwards and forwards night after night. It isn't
good enough.

MADGE. What do you imagine she must think of you, making
an exhibition of yourself?

FRED. I don't care.

MADGE. I believe you do it on purpose.

FRED. It's getting on my nerves the way she turns up day after
day on exactly the same cue. You could tell the time by her.

MADGE. I'm not listening to any more. You'd better go and
find that Arthur you're so fond of.

FRED (*going off*). I'll be in the back if you want me.

He exits. MADGE *powders her nose. Fade in the noise of
a children's playground.*

Enter QUEENIE.

QUEENIE. All ready?

MADGE. Just a minute. (*She fetches an umbrella from the
back of the stage.*) Now –

QUEENIE (*inhaling a deep breath*). – look at your Janice!

MADGE. I can't seem to get her to stop the habit of dusting
when she's excited.

QUEENIE. She's highly strung, that's what it is.

MADGE. She's had a nasty cold.

QUEENIE. She's looking peaky.

MADGE. Look at her now – brushing the steps. I'm thinking of having her trained.

QUEENIE. Trained?

MADGE. She's got it in her, I'm sure. (*Pause.*) I gave you a ring last night; weren't you in?

QUEENIE. It was you, was it? I heard the phone go about eight. We were watching the re-makes of those detergent adverts.

MADGE. I must keep my eyes open. He's too mean to buy the *Television Times* so we never know when anything is on. I missed Fabulous Camay yesterday.

QUEENIE. What a shame. (*Absently.*) You didn't miss *her*, did you?

MADGE (*surprised*). Was *she* on?

QUEENIE. My word, yes.

MADGE. And you saw her?

QUEENIE. We were so excited. She was on a horse.

MADGE. What kind of a horse?

QUEENIE. Big made, you know. And black.

MADGE. Black? She seems to go for *big* BLACK –

QUEENIE. – horses. Yes.

MADGE. She works so hard, poor thing. I'm sure she overdoes it.

QUEENIE. Do you really think so? Do you really think so?

MADGE. I'm sure she does. I only hope she won't –

QUEENIE. I'm sure she won't.

MADGE. What I think is so nice is she's just the same as you and me. I feel she gets up in the morning feeling a couple of degrees under just like us.

QUEENIE. And *more*.

MADGE. When her sister got married she didn't bat an eyelid, did she?

QUEENIE. She certainly did not.

MADGE. She didn't bat an eyelid; though you and I noticed a thing or two. Though we noticed the way the wind blew. She takes after her granny. SHE was a grand old –

QUEENIE. Lady, SHE was.

MADGE. A real –

QUEENIE. Lady –

MADGE. With a heart of gold and a –

QUEENIE. – to match. Yes, yes. She was a lady. I don't think ordinary people could hazard a guess whether –

MADGE. Truth is certainly stranger than fiction. But I like them. They're a grand lot. So homely. You feel they're just like US.

Silence.

QUEENIE. Her auntie was a nice woman. It came as a big shock to me when I heard she'd passed over. A big shock. She'd always been my favourite. Didn't she look impressive in her uniform?

MADGE. It suited her.

QUEENIE. It brought her out.

MADGE. Her auntie's hubby is some kind of a relation of her hubby, isn't he?

QUEENIE. Do you think that's wise?

MADGE. I'm all against it myself, though they seem to be managing.

QUEENIE. If you read between the lines.

MADGE. Her hubby must be a sport to have around. They must get on well together, because she's the same, you know?

QUEENIE. – just the same.

MADGE. She only looks at home with a scarf over her perm at a race-course, or watching polo, or cricket. She clearly never has an intelligent thought in her head (and neither does he for that matter) and that's what I like to see.

QUEENIE. Oh, well, naturally. It runs in the family, doesn't it? They can't help the way they're made, can they?

MADGE. And what about her mother?

QUEENIE. What about her mother? What about her mother? I don't know.

MADGE. Her mother and her sister's hubby seem as thick as thieves.

QUEENIE. NO!

MADGE. I don't say for a minute –

QUEENIE. Oh, I'm sure you must be mistaken –

MADGE. She wouldn't like that at all, would she? I'd say she wouldn't. I'd say she wouldn't. And yet, if the worst came to the worst, she'd take it in her stride. She is a miracle. No one but her . . . no one else in the world . . . could draw such crowds, attract such cheers and win such warm affection. For she is the only person in the WORLD whose grace and charm cut through race, creed, religion and politics. Why everyone has a soft spot for her. WITHOUT EXCEPTION. The whole world shares the ideals she represents. And that's what I always say. She's a trouper. She's one of the best. SHE IS A LADY. I'll say she is. And don't you let me catch any of you forgetting it.

Silence.

QUEENIE (*shaking her head*). I can't get over you missing her.

MADGE. I don't know how it happened.

QUEENIE. You, of all people. You're usually so keen. You never miss a single episode, do you?

MADGE. Never, apart from illness. I've never missed an episode. I must be slipping.

QUEENIE. You must be slipping.

MADGE. I've a lot on my mind.

QUEENIE. Worries?

MADGE. Yes.

QUEENIE. Private matter?

MADGE. It's him.

QUEENIE. What's the matter with him?

MADGE. I don't know. Everything seems too much trouble. Like the lamp-post. Look at him now, where is he? (*She crosses the stage and calls.*) Fred!

QUEENIE. He's in the back with Arthur.

MADGE. All he ever thinks of is messing about with Arthur.

QUEENIE. What are we going to do? (*Shivers.*) It's cold out here.

MADGE. I'm going inside; it's not my business.

Enter WEBBER.

WEBBER. Anything wrong?

MADGE. He's gone and left the place to look after itself.

WEBBER. As a matter of fact I want to be alone for a few minutes –

MADGE. You're always covering up. One of these days you won't be here – and what will he do then?

WEBBER. Excuse me. (*He looks out front.*) Hallo, I was hoping you'd turn up.

SYKES (*from the audience*). I apologise for being late.

WEBBER. Quite all right. Quite all right. Won't you step up
here?

SYKES. Is it in order?

WEBBER. You don't mind, do you Madge?

MADGE. Me? Why should I care? Oh! this wind! I'm going
inside out of it.

WEBBER. If you see him anywhere around, send him out
here.

Exit MADGE *and* QUEENIE. SYKES *climbs to the stage
level.*

WEBBER. Good. We shall have the place to ourselves.
(*Pause.*) Did you have any trouble finding us?

SYKES. Not a bit. Everyone knows this theatre.

WEBBER. We're quite a landmark. Yes, *quite* a little landmark. (*Pause.*) Are you enjoying yourself?

SYKES. I don't dislike the play. It's charming, really
charming – the young woman who plays the wife gives
a fine performance.

WEBBER. And yet, you know, I had to speak to her only last
night for missing an entrance.

SYKES. It must be difficult to judge when to make one.

WEBBER. Not at all.

SYKES. Oh, I don't know. It must be difficult to time the
exact moment when to break in on a scene.

Enter FRED.

FRED. Did you want me? oh, am I butting in?

SYKES. That illustrates my point.

WEBBER. Quite, quite. (*To* FRED.) You misjudged an
entrance. If you hadn't come in we would have carried on
without you. So your entrance wasn't necessary.

FRED. Sorry. Shall I try again?

WEBBER. Later, perhaps. You'd better make the change. We're freezing out here.

FRED *removes the lamp-post and exits.*

SYKES. He's the husband, isn't he?

WEBBER. Yes. Her husband. He was a replacement. We had a bit of trouble with the previous one. Frank – that was his name. An unpleasant business.

SYKES. Is it personal?

FRED *enters dragging on a ramp. He exits and brings on a bath and three sieves.*

WEBBER (*lowering his voice*). You see, Madge said this Frank was too young to be her husband. We had to let him go.

SYKES. How embarrassing.

WEBBER. It's all in the day's work. (*Looks at his watch.*) Well, now I'll just give you a rough outline of the story. Madge and Fred have been married for twelve years; during that time they've had their ups and downs like any other couple, but on the whole they've been happy and contented. They have a delightful daughter called Janice. (*Confidentially.*) I'm Uncle Bill to young Janice. And I'll let you into a secret – we're engaged! She proposed to me in her mummy's dressing room before the show. Delightful! So naive! And completely unspoiled by success. It hasn't affected her a jot. Not a jot. She's still the simple little girl she was before the play opened. (*Pause.*) Ah, that's better. quite a difference. We're out of that cold wind now. (*He unloosens his scarf and takes off his gloves.*) Janice's Daddy, Fred, has become obsessed by the idea that his life is being wasted. This threatens to endanger his marriage. Now, you've seen, haven't you, Madge and Fred at home? Next we'll show you them at work – oh, yes, Madge is a busy modern housewife, does two jobs a day, and so she can't be expected to put up with her husband in the evening, can she? If you'll go back to your seat . . .

SYKES *does so.*

Are you settled?

SYKES. Yes.

WEBBER. ☐Excellent. Excellent. Then, if you don't mind we
could begin.

SYKES. I'm ready for you.

WEBBER. Ready for us? It is we who are ready for you.
We're at your service.

Blackout.

Lights up on FRED *pushing a boulder before him up the
ramp. A* SMALL PART PLAYER *enters with a notebook
and pencil.*

SPP. You seem to have a really worthwhile job here.

FRED. We have our coats off, sir. Work is recognised as a
virtue.

SPP. You push this stone –

FRED. Up the hill, sir.

SPP. And what happens then?

FRED. It all depends. It should roll down again. But accidents
will happen. Sometimes it topples over the other side.

SPP. Tell me, what made you take up this work?

FRED. The security, sir. And I did want to be a useful member
of society. I've worked here since I left school. Twenty-four
years, I've worked at this job. Twenty-four years.

SPP. That's good to hear.

FRED. Almost half-way. In another twenty-six years – not
long is it, sir? – in twenty-six years I'll be able to retire.
I'm making exciting plans for my retirement, sir.

SPP. It won't be long now.

FRED. It isn't long. Oh, the young people of today don't know
what they're missing. They turn up their noses at jobs like
this which offer security.

SPP. The industry is failing to attract youth?

FRED. Yes sir, yes. The industry is definitely failing to attract the youth of today.

SPP. Why do you think this is?

FRED. There are many reasons. First I think the young people of today want a job with more glamour. Though this is a rewarding job, sir. We have an excellent pension scheme. When I retire I shall be given a present by the firm, *and* a pension, *and* references in case I should take up part-time work during my retirement.

SPP. I see you have the whole thing at your fingertips.

FRED. I've given the matter a lot of thought.

SPP. Does your wife go out to work?

FRED. Yes, sir. She has a job which is stimulating, interesting and, above all, a benefit to society.

Lights out on FRED. *Lights up on* MADGE, QUEENIE *and* GLADYS. *They are dressed in white overalls and are attempting to catch water from the bath in sieves.*

MADGE. Hallo, Queenie, I didn't know you worked here.

QUEENIE. I'm deputising for Enid, she's being taken to court over not paying her telly licence.

MADGE. What a thing to happen.

QUEENIE. She's been asking for it.

GLADYS. There's only one thing I dread –

QUEENIE. We can all guess; it's Short Time.

GLADYS. Imagine! only four hundred sievefulls a day instead of eight hundred.

MADGE. It may never happen.

| QUEENIE. } | God's good. |
| MADGE.   } | Look on the bright side. |

| GLADYS. } | Take the rough with the smooth. |
| QUEENIE. } | Into each life some rain must fall. |

GLADYS. I couldn't bear to be in one of these dead-end jobs. I like to feel I'm doing something useful.

MADGE. I know what you mean.

GLADYS. I'm helping to make the world go round –

Silence.

QUEENIE. Enid's mum was ever so shocked about Enid being taken to court.

MADGE. There you are. Pride goes before a fall.

GLADYS. I keep thinking of shorter hours. What if they stopped the overtime?

QUEENIE. Oh, don't!

GLADYS. And put us on shorter hours.

MADGE. Look out, Glad! some of the holes in your sieve are blocked. You'll be catching water in it if you don't watch yourself.

GLADYS. Thanks for the warning. (*She takes out a nail file and unblocks the holes.*) I think I'd go mad if they put us on shorter hours. Nothing to do. Sitting around the house all day. It'd drive me off my rocker.

QUEENIE. Yes.

MADGE. We all do a good day's work and the pay is good.

QUEENIE. It is.

GLADYS. I worry about my Sandra. She wants to take up – WELL! You'll think I'm out of my mind if I tell you. I'm sick with worry.

MADGE. I'd see someone if I were you.

Silence.

QUEENIE. There's something wrong.

Silence.

GLADYS. What if they came to you and said, 'Next week you're to be allowed four hundred sievefulls and that's your lot?'

QUEENIE. Don't!

MADGE. Do shut up, Glad, you're getting on my nerves.

GLADYS. Shorter hours will come. I'm certain.

QUEENIE. The Grain-Sorters are on short time.

GLADYS. Imagine getting up in the morning and not being
    able to go to work!

MADGE. You'll make your life a misery if you go on like this.

GLADYS. I can't help it.

A pause while all three sieve silently for a minute or two.

GLADYS. My Sandra's a big worrit.

MADGE. When does she leave school?

GLADYS. July.

MADGE. She won a scholarship didn't she?

GLADYS. Oh, yes. She's got it in her, there's no doubt. I think
    that's what's at the back of it. (*Pause. In confidence.*) She
    wants to be bound to a wheel and to go careering on and
    on round and round until the day she drops.

QUEENIE. That's a funny job for a woman.

GLADYS. Exactly. My own sentiments. I put all the
    arguments in favour of taking a nice, sensible job – like
    this.

| QUEENIE. } | It's secure. |
| MADGE.   } | It's steady. |

| QUEENIE. } | Prospects are good. |
| MADGE.   } | The industry is expanding. |

| QUEENIE. } | A bonus scheme; lunch vouchers. |
| MADGE.   } | A Sport's Club; recreational facilities. |

GLADYS. It's no good. The Wheel is all she cares about.

QUEENIE. It's a man's profession.

MADGE. It's not easy for women to get jobs on the Wheel.

QUEENIE. Jobs for women are scarce. Whereas the chances
of women making a success of water-sieving are good.

GLADYS. Why are all the Wheelers men?

QUEENIE. And the Straw-Spinners?

GLADYS. And the Cloud-Predictors?

MADGE. And Apple-Graspers, and Oath-Takers and Corpse-
Judgers?

Silence.

GLADYS. I don't know which way to turn.

QUEENIE. Well, I call it a –

MADGE. – silly idea –

QUEENIE. You've spoiled her, Glad –

MADGE. – spared the rod –

QUEENIE. – and spoiled the child.

MADGE. And God only knows you've done that. Spoiled her
until she thinks she's the mistress of the house and not you.
Now if I were in your shoes I'd put her in the Winding-
Sheet business.

GLADYS. It's more than my life's worth to suggest it.

MADGE. You won't find a nicer job.

GLADYS. It's the night-work; she just won't listen. If it means
the night-shift she's –

QUEENIE. She's spoilt.

GLADYS. It's her being a girl after boys; a rose between two
thorns they said when she was born.

MADGE. You've made your bed and you must lie on it.

A bell rings loudly.

QUEENIE. Five and twenty past! How time flies.

MADGE. Thank God it's Saturday tomorrow. I'm no friend of the man who invented work.

GLADYS. What would we do without it?

They form a queue at the clock holding clock-cards in their hands. The dialogue is played as they wait for the clock to reach five-thirty.

QUEENIE. Anna Neagle's on tonight.

GLADYS. – lovely *she* was.

MADGE. – lovely. Yes, lovely. I remember her years ago.

GLADYS. Years ago.

MADGE. I remember her.

QUEENIE. Did you see the original?

GLADYS. No, not the original. I saw the revival after the war.

QUEENIE. Yes, they did a revival, I believe.

GLADYS. Oh, yes. How old do you take me for? See the original? My mother saw the original. But I saw it when they revived her.

A clock strikes the half-hour.

GLADYS. Here! where's the clock?

VOICES IN THE QUEUE. Come on, Glad, what are you playing at? We want to get home sometime tonight.

GLADYS. What have they done?

VOICES. Get a move on. What's the matter with you? Don't you want to leave, Glad?

Enter FRED, out of breath, pushing a clock.

MADGE. About time too.

QUEENIE. Never mind, dear, we all love you.

They clock out.

MADGE. I suppose you'll be home about six?

FRED. They've asked me to do overtime.

MADGE. You'd better. It'll come in handy for Janice's new shoes. I'll keep your dinner hot.

FRED *removes the bath and the sieves and ramp. He brings on the two chairs and puts the lamp-post between them in the position of the standard lamp of the opening scene.*

Light on MADGE *and* QUEENIE.

MADGE. He needs a tonic. Maybe he'd be more cheerful. But the funny thing is he's not interested; everybody ought to be interested in tonics at his age. So morbid he's getting too. We were having a constitutional in the recreation ground at the weekend, and he passed the men playing bowls – well, live and let live, I always say, bowls passes the time. 'You'd think they'd find something better to do,' he says. And the man got quite upset. 'You'll be dead soon.' Dead. And Death. That's all he thinks of. They weren't doing any harm, having a game of bowls. He told me they gave him the pip; nothing on their minds except the rates and no pleasures except the pools and the latest case of incest in the papers. So *he* says. They're not even alive, at least not what anyone who was alive would call alive. They're dead. But you can't go around telling people they're dead without annoying them, can you?

QUEENIE. He needs a good tonic; try him on Parish's Food, that's good.

QUEENIE *exits.* MADGE *sits in a chair. The doorbell rings. She gets up and goes off. Sound of door slamming. She re-enters with* WEBBER.

MADGE. He's not home yet.

WEBBER. He's late, isn't he?

MADGE. They asked him to do overtime.

WEBBER (*pause*). How's life treating you?

MADGE. So, so.

WEBBER. Like that is it?

MADGE. I'm under the weather; it's the time of year.

WEBBER. How's that daughter of yours?

MADGE. Janice? I've put her to bed, she's had a tiring day. We're having her trained, you know?

WEBBER. Are you?

MADGE. It was his idea. I wasn't too keen. There you are. A proud father and all that.

WEBBER *notices the lamp-post between the two chairs.*

WEBBER. Hallo, was this his idea?

MADGE (*seeing it for the first time*). Oh – I copied it from one of the women's magazines. Like it?

WEBBER. Hm. Did it cost much?

MADGE. No more than an ordinary lamp, and the litter basket comes in handy.

WEBBER. We must keep up with the times.

MADGE. We must be modern.

WEBBER. Up to date. (*Looks at his watch.*) He *is* late.

Silence. WEBBER *comes to the edge of the stage.*

WEBBER. Everything OK?

SYKES. I'd like a drink.

WEBBER. We'll do a few cuts then. (*To* MADGE.) Miss the scene in the park, and the one in the launderette, and the one where Janice gets lost, and the one where Fred threatens to leave you for the first time.

MADGE. What about the scene where I leave him?

WEBBER. Cut that. Cut the one where Janice has her first exam, and the one where the bats escape, and the one where Queenie brings you and Fred together.

MADGE. If you say so. (*Pause. As* WEBBER *exits.*) You can find your own way out, can you?

WEBBER. Yes.

Exit.

MADGE *sits down.* FRED *enters. He sits down.*

FRED. Are we in the mood for talking?

MADGE. Where have you been?

FRED. Out. (*Pause.*) I'm going to leave you.

MADGE. Why?

FRED. I'm bored.

MADGE. You have no reason to be.

FRED. I'm bored with the way you open the door. I'm bored
with the way you get into bed. I'm bored with the way you
get out of bed. And the way you use the bed. I'm bored
with the pillowslips, and the counterpane, and the sheets
and the eiderdown. I'm bored with that picture of a cat's
wedding hanging over the bed, and I'm going to smash the
alarm clock which plays 'Oh, What a Beautiful Morning'
beside the bed!

MADGE. No you won't.

FRED. I will. Where have you put it? You've hidden it.

MADGE. Oh! Oh, dear! Fred! Fred! Don't do it. We shan't be
able to wake up. I'm frightened, I've never seen you like
this. I like the clock.

FRED. I hate it.

MADGE. It's cheerful. I like 'Oh, What a Beautiful Morning'.

FRED. Cheerful?

MADGE. Cheerful, yes.

FRED. Not for me.

MADGE. Why not?

FRED. Because it's morning, that's why. Because it's seven
o'clock, that's why. Where is it? I'm going to smash it.

MADGE. Leave it alone. I won't have you behaving like this.

You'll wake Janice.

FRED. I'm going to smash it to hell. (*Pause*.) Smash it. Smash it. All those wheels going round and round and round –

MADGE. The craftsmanship takes your breath away. It's a work of art.

FRED. – round and round and round; eating my life away. And the dome on top with the dancer inside.

MADGE. Think of the time it took to make anything so perfect!

FRED. I'm going to smash the dome with the dancer inside. Smash it. Smash it. Smash those bleeding little wheels.

MADGE. It's a lovely piece of work. So elaborate. So decorative.

FRED. In the morning I hear it playing, and I get up –

MADGE. – you get up.

FRED. I stretch myself.

MADGE. And I say, What time is it, dear? (*Pause*.) It's a sacred moment.

FRED. Then –

MADGE. – you say –

FRED. – about seven, dear.

MADGE. So kind you always are to me. It must take a lot of patient searching to find the time. You're a good husband. Nothing is too much trouble. (*Pause*.) Well, carry on.

FRED. I put on my shirt.

MADGE. You've no idea of the funny feeling I get inside as I watch you take off your pyjama jacket. I watch too long. I've been over-exciting myself lately. That's why I'm so tired all day.

FRED. And then –

MADGE. – then –

FRED (*quickly*). Then I take off my trousers!

MADGE. I never dare to look. It's so personal. I close my eyes and hear you say –

FRED. – two lumps as usual, dear?

MADGE. Yes. You say –

FRED. – two lumps as usual, dear.

MADGE. We lead a deeply human life. There's no getting away from it. So moving and quietly sincere.

FRED (*pause*). I'm beginning to get excited by it.

MADGE. I knew you would. I knew you'd be struck by the solemnity of everyday life.

FRED. The Formality! I'd never realised.

MADGE. It's classical in its simplicity. (*Pause*.) Oh, the beauty of it, dear, the beauty of it. Have you ever considered that? We're not just part of a mass, you and I. No. We're joined to a living integral whole, a warm, pulsating body bound together; you, me, and Mr Macmillan and Mr Lennox-Boyd and Lord Hailsham and Mr Cotton and Mr Clore, all bound together in a wonderful experience called LIVING. (*Pause*.) So – poetic – don't you think?

FRED (*amazed*). Madge, dear, Madge.

MADGE. You didn't know I had a touch of the –

FRED. Madge.

MADGE. – poet, did you dear?

FRED. Madge.

MADGE. You didn't know I had that side. It's the –

FRED. Madge.

MADGE. – dark of the moon. Everyone is a moon and has a dark side which they show to no one.

FRED. Madge!

MADGE. These are the quiet thoughts that come to me in the

morning as I wait for you to bring me my cup of tea –

FRED. – with two lumps of sugar.

MADGE. – small lumps, yes.

FRED (*impressed*). Your cup of tea!

MADGE. I've revealed new and unsuspected realms of imagination, of unique and lasting value in our marriage. These little thoughts of mine, and much more, show my awed recognition of the mystery at the heart of *life*.

FRED. Life.

MADGE. – life –

FRED. Life.

MADGE. – life –

FRED. – the poetry and savagery of it! Oh!

Silence.

MADGE (*reminding him*). And you go –

FRED. – down the stairs. And I see the holes in the carpet, and the stain on the wall where Janice upset her po, and the green paint on the banisters.

MADGE. The mat in the hall; the letter box.

FRED. – with the morning paper pushed through it.

MADGE. It's an experience, seeing our hall in the dawn, as the sun rises. All that light coming ninety-three million miles through space to shine on our Welcome mat.

FRED. And the barometer Queenie gave us as a wedding present.

MADGE. And the shoe cupboard.

FRED. And the stair-rods from Woolworths.

MADGE. And the picture from the Medici gallery.

FRED. It makes you think. (*Pause.*) Ninety-three million miles through space to shine on our kitchen and the cups you forgot to wash the night before.

MADGE. When we win the pools I'm going to buy a machine to do it. We'll have no bother any more.

FRED. Think of the millions who don't win every week; millions like us.

MADGE. I'm desperately concerned about the money; desperately concerned.

FRED. What good is the money if your heart is broken?

MADGE. Will it make us hard? I keep asking myself, will it alter our lives: our unhurried way of life?

FRED. Will it make us bitter?

MADGE. The cocktails and laughter; will they spoil us?

FRED. I couldn't stand it if we were spoiled.

MADGE. We must make a determined effort not to let our new-found wealth affect us – but we must have serviettes with our meals. Now that's a thing I shall insist on.

FRED. It doesn't bring happiness.

MADGE. No.

FRED. The rich are probably as poor as we are if truth were only known.

MADGE. Oh, dear!

FRED. What good is wealth if you're living a life that's a mockery?

MADGE. Oh, dear!

FRED. If you never know who's your friend? Is it worth it? If you don't know which way to turn? You have a big house and grounds and servants and holidays in the south of France and all the time there's bitterness and regret in your heart; poor little rich girl, that's what you'll be. It's not worth the risk.

MADGE. You're trying to put me off.

FRED. Those weekends at Mrs Gerald Legge's and the horses and you'll never look right in a Dior – and if you put two and two together with Uffa Fox you'll be seasick. And then there's the entertaining –

MADGE. You make it sound awful.

FRED. – a terrible lot of entertaining there'll be, and bridge and the Chelsea Flower Show and Church on Sunday and Scotland for the grouse; you know how you hate them –

MADGE. Please stop.

FRED. I'll have to wear a bowler and carry a tightly rolled umbrella; what will the neighbours say?

MADGE. 1 don't know what's the matter with you, you've never been like this before.

FRED. I'm warning you.

MADGE. I get so tired of it all, so desperately tired. I'm unhappy.

FRED. Why?

MADGE. You're leaving me.

FRED. It's this social whirl; I'm not used to it. There's the Royal Enclosure, and Janice – she'll be coming out soon.

MADGE. Fred!

FRED. We'll have to go to a Garden Party. And it's so difficult to get floral gowns and those big hats – and what about grass stains on your gloves, eh? Have you thought about them? I don't suppose you have. That's your trouble. Thoughtless. It's almost impossible to get grass stains from white gloves.

MADGE. I won't go then.

FRED. Won't go! Do you know what you're saying?

MADGE. I'm not being made a fool of.

FRED. And how do you think Janice will feel? It's not as if she asks a favour every day. What chance has she got of

being voted 'Deb of the Year' if you behave like this?
You'll ruin her first season if you're not careful.

MADGE. Don't let me stop you going. I'm sure you're dying
to be with the others.

Silence.

FRED. I suppose we could try Thawpit.

MADGE. You care more about those gloves than you do about
me.

Enter WEBBER carrying an alarm clock which is ringing.

WEBBER. For Heaven's sake! get on with it! We'll be here all
night.

Exit.

MADGE (*hastily*). Goodbye then.

FRED. I'll always love you.

MADGE. It's a pity we couldn't make a go of it.

FRED. I'm going to kiss you, and then I want you to turn
away. You won't see me leave.

MADGE. What a nice idea.

FRED. Do you like it?

MADGE. It suits you down to the ground.

FRED. It's not an original.

MADGE. I think it's every bit as good; nobody could tell the
difference.

She turns. He kisses her on the neck and exits.

MADGE. Queenie and that friend of hers had a nasty
experience yesterday. They were walking down the road
when one of Queenie's heels came off. She could have
broken her neck, she fell from such a height. (*Pause.*)
Take care of yourself dear. I know you're not here any
more so I can break down. (*Cries.*) Fred – Fred –

Enter WEBBER. *He walks to the edge of the stage and speaks briskly to* SYKES.

WEBBER. There! that's over with. Now if you want a drink, follow me.

They make an exit to the bar. Lights up.

Exit.

The curtain does not fall.

End of Act One.

ACT TWO

The stage is as at the end of Act One. After the fire-curtain has risen, SYKES *comes hurriedly from the bar, or the direction of the bar, and climbs to the stage level.* WEBBER *enters and they remove everything onstage. They bring on two single beds and a locker and a wooden chair of the kind used in hospitals. Inside the locker are two bunches of flowers which* WEBBER *removes and takes offstage, and a water jug and two glasses which he places on top of the locker.*

Fade house lights. Silence. WEBBER *sits on a bed and mops his brow.*

WEBBER. The staff problem gets worse.

SYKES. Fred left then?

WEBBER. Good God, yes! We haven't heard a word from him since Madge got her divorce.

SYKES. How is she?

WEBBER. Not too bad, all things considered. He never writes, you know. She got a card one Christmas to say he'd taken a job abroad. (*Pause*.) Did you ever meet her father?

SYKES. Can't say I remember.

WEBBER. He's in hospital, not expected to see the year out. (*Pause*.) And Queenie – you remember her?

SYKES. I should think I do.

WEBBER. She married an Indian. There was a lot of talk, I can tell you. She's going to Sutpura with him. Entering his harem and all that. She signed the papers. (*Pause*.) And Gladys – she was the one with the glasses – Gladys passed away a couple of years ago. Dropped dead at work. Strained herself everyone said. (*Pause*.) And that's all from me. What have you to say for yourself?

SYKES. I spent my time in the bar over the way.

WEBBER (*shocked*). The last five years? In a bar? You must be soaking it up.

SYKES. There you are. Mustn't complain, I suppose.

WEBBER. Seen a doctor?

SYKES. Dozens of them.

WEBBER. I hope you'll be able to give me a hand – a bit of lifting? Good. Here we go again.

WEBBER *and* SYKES *exit.*

Sound of visitors arriving. The SMALL PART PLAYER *crosses the stage dressed as a nurse.*

Enter FRED *and* MADGE, *who each get into a bed. They both settle down, mutter to themselves, and turn over. He sits up and reaches for the water jug. She does the same. An orchestra somewhere strikes up a romantic little tune. Reaching for the water, they see one another.*

MADGE. What are *you* doing here?

FRED. A bit of an accident on my way to get married; I ought to be on my honeymoon.

MADGE. So should I.

FRED. What happened?

MADGE. We had an accident too. The church roof came in on top of us.

FRED. That's the trouble with churches nowadays; it's suicide to enter them. (*Pause.*) How is Janice keeping?

MADGE. She polishes beautifully. She's a born Cleansing Agent. So talented! (*Pause.*) Listen! Our tune!

FRED. I know.

Silence.

FRED. Have you known – him – for long?

MADGE. About six years. I never realised his feelings until
a few months ago. (*Pause.*) It was a whirlwind courtship,
when I took Janice to Norfolk to convalesce.

FRED. Norfolk?

MADGE. Yes.

FRED. Very hilly Norfolk.

MADGE. Hills! – oh! the climbing we had to do. Up and
down, up and down, all day long. I got worried for Janice's
health. She's been poorly lately.

FRED. Ill?

MADGE. She overtaxed her strength working for this carpet
beating exam she's so keen on passing. (*Pause.*) What
about – her – you didn't tell me her name.

FRED. Susan.

MADGE. How old is she?

FRED. Sixteen last week.

MADGE (*pause*). I do think – I do think you might have
waited. She'll hardly have had time to mature.

FRED. She's a big girl. (*Pause.*) How old is –

MADGE. Jimmy.

FRED. How old is Jimmy?

MADGE. Sixty-one.

FRED (*incredulous*). Sixty-one! (*Pause.*) I'd never have
believed it. You, of all people, going around with that type
of man.

MADGE. He's very dynamic.

FRED. He must be.

MADGE. That's what first attracted me to him. We were doing
a spot of climbing –

FRED. – in Norfolk –

MADGE. Yes. We were more or less amusing ourselves, Janice and I, until she lost her alpenstock, and we found ourselves stranded. With night coming on, and reports of avalanches, we were terrified, when, out of nowhere, came Jimmy. Suave, immaculate, devil-may-care, the epitome of all that a lonely woman could desire. *And* he had two alpenstocks. So he loaned one to Janice and helped us back to the chalet. (*Pause.*) He proposed to me next day.

Silence. The music plays on.

FRED. I've gone off that tune.

Silence.

MADGE. What have you been doing lately; you never write.

FRED. I joined the Merchant Navy.

MADGE. Like it?

FRED. Not much.

MADGE. China must be interesting.

FRED. We called at Hong Kong once. I didn't go ashore, though.

MADGE. And Japan.

FRED. Some of the lads enjoyed it.

MADGE. Did you go to India? And see the Taj Mahal?

FRED. Oh, yes! now that is something special. It's unbeliev-able – like a huge biscuit box. You'd have loved it.

Silence.

MADGE. Queenie married an Indian chap, did you hear?

FRED. Yes.

MADGE. She's leaving soon to take up residence in the Palace of the Mogul Emperors at Sutpura. I can't fancy the place myself, but she's looking forward to it. (*Pause.*) She wanted to take young Janice, because there'll be all those rooms to clean. I wouldn't hear of it. Janice is at the start of her career; it wouldn't be fair to her. (*Pause.*) What's the good of a Diploma in polishing if the floors are made of stone? No sense in it. So I put my foot down.

FRED. When is Queenie leaving?

MADGE. The end of the year. She's taking lessons in nude-dancing, and getting used to cobras – we have the spare room full of them.

FRED. Have you?

MADGE. I thought that'd interest you.

FRED. Remember the bats?

MADGE. Shall I ever forget the trouble we had when they escaped?

FRED. I'm sorry, dear.

MADGE. I never regret our marriage, Fred.

The SMALL PART PLAYER *enters with two thermometers, which he puts into their mouths.*

SPP (*taking the thermometer out again*). You're OK now, Fred.

FRED. Can I get up?

SPP. Nothing wrong with *you.*

FRED *exits. The* SMALL PART PLAYER *tidies the bed.*

SPP. Let me just have a look at that thermometer. (*Does so.*) You'll have to stay in for a few days longer.

MADGE. When is visiting day?

SPP. Why? Are you expecting anyone?

MADGE. Fred promised to look in.

Enter FRED *with a bunch of flowers. Exit the* SMALL PART PLAYER.

FRED. Hallo, dear, feeling better?

MADGE. I am now. What lovely flowers!

FRED. They are nice, aren't they? I'll leave them here. Nurse can see to them.

MADGE. How was the wedding?

FRED. We put it off; Susan's down with jaundice.

MADGE. What a shame.

Enter WEBBER *also with a bunch of flowers.*

MADGE. Jimmy! I thought you couldn't make it?

WEBBER. I wangled half-an-hour.

MADGE. Look who's here.

WEBBER. Fred! when did you blow in?

MADGE. A few days ago.

FRED. Long time no see?

MADGE. He's getting married soon.

WEBBER. Married, eh? Try and try again?

Silence.

FRED. So you're the Jimmy I've heard so much about?

WEBBER. Surprised?

FRED. I certainly am.

Silence.

WEBBER. You've given up the Merchant Navy then?

FRED. For the time being.

WEBBER. Care to have your old job back? We could do with
an extra hand; someone with experience.

FRED. I'll take it on for a trial run.

WEBBER. Suits me.

FRED. When would you like me to start?

WEBBER. No time like the present. You'll find Sykes outside,
he'll put you in the picture. (*Exit* FRED.) I'm having to get
rid of Sykes. Drinks like a fish. Can't leave the stuff alone.
Do you know, he spent the best part of five years in a bar?
Shocking really.

MADGE. I'm sorry for his poor wife, what a time she must have.

Enter SYKES.

SYKES. I'm off then.

WEBBER. Don't forget the little job you promised to do, will you?

SYKES. No.

He exits to his seat in the audience, slightly drunk.

WEBBER. He reeks of whisky!

MADGE. He can't help it.

WEBBER. Perhaps you're right. (*Pause.*) I've brought these for you.

MADGE. Aren't they lovely! Leave them there. Nurse will know what to do with them.

Silence.

WEBBER (*tenderly*). How are you, my darling?

MADGE. Very happy.

WEBBER. The Vicar has agreed to damages.

MADGE. He was as upset as we were.

WEBBER. What if you'd been killed?

MADGE. *You* might have been killed too.

WEBBER. No danger for me, dearest. I was at the altar; it was the cherubim over the aisle which fell.

MADGE. My gown – my lovely gown! (*Bursts into tears.*)

WEBBER. There, dear, there! We'll get another every bit as good. As long as you are safe.

He takes her in his arms. Slow fade. Enter FRED *with a chair. He places it in position and fetches the other. MADGE gets out of bed and exits, returning dressed. She sits in one of the chairs and remains seated until she is needed.*

WEBBER. Ready for work? That's what I like to see.

FRED. Could you lend me a hand with the beds?

> WEBBER *and* FRED *remove the beds, the locker and flowers, etc., and bring on the standard lamp, and any wedding presents which may be mentioned later. Enter downstage* QUEENIE *and the actress who played* GLADYS.

QUEENIE. Excuse me for saying this, but how is it you look so similar to poor Gladys?

GLADYS. I'm her twin sister.

QUEENIE. That was lucky.

GLADYS. More good management than luck, if you ask me.

QUEENIE (*impressed*). You've got Gladys's manner to a T! Why announce her death? You could have stepped in, and no one would have been the wiser.

GLADYS. There you are. That's the way it goes.

QUEENIE. What's your name?

GLADYS. Gladys.

QUEENIE. What a coincidence.

> *Silence.*

GLADYS. Now it's my turn to ask the questions. Are there any vacancies?

QUEENIE. What do you mean?

GLADYS. You let something out back there. Not much, but enough for me to gather that there might be one or two jobs going. I could see you didn't want to talk then –

QUEENIE. I still don't.

GLADYS. You mustn't be like that.

QUEENIE. It's a personal matter.

GLADYS (*admiringly*). You're a dark horse, Queenie, and no mistake.

QUEENIE. I'll say this for you, you're out for what's going.

GLADYS. Here, steady on! I've got my feelings. Nobody likes to be insulted, and to their face.

QUEENIE. A joke's a joke.

GLADYS. I wouldn't have brought it up in the normal way, but I'm getting tired of water-sieving day after day, week after week, and I can't face grain-sorting or unpicking shrouds, or apple-grasping; and wheeling and straw-spinning and feather-painting and cloud-predicting are men's jobs. I'd try over-reaching myself but I'm not an educated woman. So I thought a job in a harem might suit me down to the ground.

QUEENIE. He's only advertising for concubines.

GLADYS. Beggars can't be choosers.

QUEENIE. You'd have to see Ramakrishna.

GLADYS. Can you fix me an appointment?

QUEENIE. I'll do my best.

GLADYS. You're an angel, Queenie.

Exit GLADYS.

Lights up on MADGE. QUEENIE *walks into the light and sits upon a chair.* SYKES *makes his way from the audience.*

QUEENIE. Gladys went to a Catholic wedding last week; she said it was like a funfair.

MADGE. They're so passionate.

QUEENIE. The first time she'd been invited to one, and oh! my –

MADGE. They make such a lot of it.

QUEENIE. People coming and going and putting money in the box and lighting candles –

MADGE. What I might call –

QUEENIE. She said she thought they'd set the place afire.

MADGE. – what I might call unrestrained.

QUEENIE. What? I'll say.

MADGE (*taking up a list which says quite plainly* GUESTS). Oh, dear! Oh, dear! Such a lot of people there'll be coming to the wedding. Where are we going to seat them?

QUEENIE. I always say there's nothing like a C of E wedding for sheer SACREDNESS, and –

MADGE. I can see someone having his wedding breakfast in the loo.

QUEENIE. HOLY QUIET.

MADGE. Yes.

QUEENIE (*absently. She examines the presents*). Ramakrishna can't be here, he's had to go and organise a tiger shoot for somebody. What are these? – sugar tongs?

MADGE. They are nice.

QUEENIE. Asparagus tongs. You never eat any.

MADGE. It's a nice thought; it's the thought that matters.

QUEENIE. You have some lovely presents. When did these come?

MADGE. By registered post.

QUEENIE. A wig-scraper, six demon spoons, a stuffed owl, a nanny-goat's postiche, an ear (oh, you are lucky, it's got a flea in it), a fully automatic oubliette, an artificial chin, a yard of linoleum –

MADGE. That once belonged to Sir Malcolm Sargent.

QUEENIE. Who sent this wicker coffin?

MADGE. Wally and Joan.

QUEENIE. It's just what you wanted!

MADGE. Don't touch the string of pearls whatever you do; Olive sent it and she forgot to wrap them in greaseproof paper.

Silence. SYKES *climbs to the stage level and sits down.*

QUEENIE. It's such a pity Janice is busy at Windsor Castle. What a boon she'd be at the wedding.

MADGE. Yes.

QUEENIE. What a treasure.

MADGE (*to* SYKES). She was a waitress in her spare time, you know?

QUEENIE. She'd be a great help with plates.

MADGE. She could serve three people at once.

QUEENIE. ☐She'll have lost the knack.

MADGE. Yes.

QUEENIE. She could have laid the table very nice.

MADGE. I wish she'd oblige; give a helping hand.

QUEENIE. She was good with serviettes.

MADGE. – beautiful.

QUEENIE. It looked so easy, yet the way she did it –

MADGE. They looked so –

QUEENIE. PROFESSIONAL –

MADGE. – yet homely –

QUEENIE. So –

MADGE. ELEGANT –

QUEENIE. – yet with a careless savoir-faire. Janice is the kind of person who is a must at a wedding.

SYKES. What was your other wedding like?

MADGE. You could hardly call it a wedding last time. He had a sudden impulse and we decided to use it and get married.

SYKES. Just like that?

MADGE. Just like that.

QUEENIE. I've still got a soft spot for old Fred.

MADGE (*moving off*). Really? Why don't you invite him to tea or something? (*Exit.*)

Silence.

QUEENIE. She should never have divorced him.

SYKES. They didn't hit it off, did they?

QUEENIE. The bats came between them.

SYKES. I don't know the details.

QUEENIE. He kept vampires and she saw red because they'd had a lot of trouble with them on their honeymoon. It was in all the papers when they escaped.

SYKES. By the way, I've heard your husband will be getting his name in the papers before long.

QUEENIE. What?

SYKES. They're publishing his story in serial form; his formative years next week, how he threw the bishop to the crocodiles, and let the python loose on the Viceroy's wife, and chained his mother to the ant-hill.

QUEENIE. I can't think what's come over everybody, wanting to read about people's private affairs. What are we going to do? We must stop publication. If Fred were here he'd think of something.

She pauses, then goes to the telephone and dials. As she does so FRED *crosses the stage carrying a brightly painted kettle from which protrude the tails of several fish.* QUEENIE *replaces the receiver.*

I was going to give you a ring. Madge told me to invite you to tea.

FRED. Thanks. I'll be seeing you. (*Exit.*)

QUEENIE. We ought to do something. There's such a thing as privacy.

Enter MADGE.

MADGE. Who were you talking to?

QUEENIE. It was a wrong number.

SYKES. But would Fred sympathise? After all he's an animal
lover.

QUEENIE. Since when?

SYKES. Look at the bats.

QUEENIE. He only took up animal loving out of boredom.
Didn't he Madge?

MADGE. Oh, yes. He'd much sooner have been an animal
hater but we couldn't afford it.

Enter WEBBER.

WEBBER (*jovially*). No need to tell me what you were talking
about, I've been listening at the keyhole.

QUEENIE. I don't see why, you were perfectly welcome to
join in the conversation.

WEBBER. I know the man who runs the Sunday papers;
I worked for him once. Having heard a rumour or two,
I went to see him in his office high above the city. I had
a little chat. (*Pause.*) And I fixed everything. (*Pause.*)
There, what do you say to that?

An astonished silence.

QUEENIE (*startled. In a worried half-whispe*r). He's cut
something. I don't understand what's going on.

SYKES (*explaining*). The man who owns the Sunday papers
has threatened to publish an article of which we all
disapprove. Webber has been to see him to buy him off.
Is that right?

WEBBER. Yes.

QUEENIE. How?

WEBBER. Wait and see.

Enter the OLD MAN *dressed as a butler.*

WEBBER. What is it, Wilkins?

OLD MAN. Dr Petrie and the young lady say they'll be down directly, sir.

WEBBER. Thank you, Wilkins. Tell Winifred or Mary to look after the young lady, will you?

OLD MAN. Very good, sir. (*Exit*.)

Silence.

MADGE. I'm not satisfied that Dad is well enough to work. He's not getting any younger.

QUEENIE. It'll take him out of himself.

MADGE. It isn't right – an old man of his age, just out of hospital, having to work for his living, polishing the silver, running up and down stairs, answering the door and telephone. It isn't good enough, Queenie. You always were inconsiderate.

QUEENIE. He gets paid.

MADGE. That's beside the point.

Silence.

SYKES. Who are Dr Petrie and the young lady?

WEBBER. Harry Petrie is his name. And Grace Oldbourne. I invited them to the wedding.

MADGE. You asked people here to stay?

QUEENIE. You behave in a very high-handed manner.

MADGE. Grace Oldbourne, I'm sure I've heard of her. She's a – honestly Jimmy, you go too far! She insults people. She's an insultrix.

WEBBER. Yes.

MADGE. And a famous one.

WEBBER. It might be nice to have a few original insults at the wedding.

MADGE. Why are they coming?

WEBBER. They're a nice couple. She's an artist in her own line, and he's written a couple of books – we ought to meet more people.

MADGE. I know what it is – the Sunday papers have sent them. You can't deny it, can you?

WEBBER. No.

MADGE. Well, they can go right back again.

QUEENIE. I think it's taking a liberty. You ought to have asked permission first; it isn't fair.

WEBBER. Let me explain. When I had a talk with my old boss who runs the Sunday papers, he promised not to print Ramakrishna's life story if you would allow Dr Petrie and Miss Oldbourne carte blanche to insult your guests, with first offers of publication.

MADGE. You must be out of your mind!

QUEENIE. It's taking a mean advantage.

MADGE. Why pick on us? Other people get married every day.

QUEENIE. Yes – why not the MacDougals? Sally MacDougal had a lovely little insult paid to her the other day – *she* won't mind.

WEBBER. There's your marriage, I think that's what the public wants; nobody cares if Miss Oldbourne insults Sally MacDougal, but if she insults a Maharanee – that's news!

MADGE. It's awful.

WEBBER. You'll try and co-operate, dear?

MADGE. Only for Queenie's sake. I know she'd never raise her head again if the crocodile story leaked out.

QUEENIE. I don't know what things are coming to.

MADGE. The best thing to do is to pretend nothing has happened. Queenie, you'd better come with me – I haven't unpacked all the presents.

WEBBER. No, no. You must wait. I daresay we shall be needed before long.

Light down, and up on DR PETRIE *and* MISS OLDBOURNE. MISS OLDBOURNE *has a box hanging from her shoulder by a strap.*

PETRIE. This is the dining room. I suppose we shall be expected to work in here?

OLDBOURNE. It looks as though we'll be able to manage one or two surprises.

PETRIE. No question of it.

OLDBOURNE. Are you intending to concentrate or to insult all and sundry?

PETRIE. You're too impatient by half, Grace. I must spy out the land first. We can't rush at these things like a bull at a gate. You know that as well as I do.

OLDBOURNE. Sorry, Harry.

PETRIE. I imagine the free-orbit insult might be called for here – it's a small wedding, nothing spectacular.

OLDBOURNE. I remember you used the free-orbit insult at the Kent wedding with some very satisfying results.

PETRIE. What a triumph!

OLDBOURNE. The peak of your career!

PETRIE. You didn't do too badly yourself.

OLDBOURNE. It was your day, though.

PETRIE. Never mind, Grace, you were the innovator. No one had thought of insulting the catering staff until you did.

OLDBOURNE. It was an accident, really.

PETRIE. An accident!

OLDBOURNE. I'd just leaned over in order to insult the bride's father when – bang! a footman bumps into me and I misfire.

PETRIE. It doesn't matter how it was done, the result was remarkable. The effect on the other guests couldn't have been calculated. It was one of those lucky breaks every insultor or insultrix prays for.

Lights up on the rest of the cast.

Oh, hello, here you are.

WEBBER. Everyone wants to welcome you.

ALL. A right royal welcome to Dr Petrie and Miss Grace.

OLDBOURNE. Thank you, thank you.

PETRIE (*to* MADGE). My colleague and I give you our heartfelt good wishes.

MADGE. You're both so kind. It's going to be nice having you.

OLDBOURNE. Charming of you to say so.

MADGE. I don't know what kind of people you usually choose – our guests are ordinary people, they have no brains to speak of – except my uncle Bob, but he'll give no trouble.

PETRIE (*making a note*). Ordinary people except B. Just a reminder.

QUEENIE. Give us a trial. Insult someone.

OLDBOURNE. I don't think –

QUEENIE. Oh, go on, just to oblige.

MADGE. I'm sure we'd all be delighted.

PETRIE. Whom shall it be?

MADGE. Anybody.

OLDBOURNE (*in a quiet professional manner to* PETRIE). Give them the all-purpose group insult.

PETRIE. I make only one stipulation – the people selected must be pig-headed enough to withstand insult; I won't have anyone seriously injured.

WEBBER. We accept your stipulation.

PETRIE. Grace, dear, you take the women, I'll take the men.

OLDBOURNE and PETRIE move to the centre of the stage. PETRIE pulls out a starter's pistol, lifts it and fires.

SYKES. Agatha Christie.

MADGE. Audrey Russell.

QUEENIE. Joan Littlewood.

WEBBER. Edith Sitwell.

OLDBOURNE. They are the biggest blow to culture since the burning of the library at Alexandria.

The whole cast applauds.

QUEENIE (*in great excitement, running to the side of the stage*). Fred! Dad! Come and watch this. Hurry or you'll miss it.

Enter the OLD MAN, GLADYS, the SMALL PART PLAYER and FRED.

QUEENIE. You must watch. I've seen nothing like it.

PETRIE lifts his starter's pistol and fires.

ALL. The BBC.

Silence.

OLDBOURNE. Extraordinary! (*Pause.*) I'm afraid –

PETRIE (*abruptly*). Be quiet, Grace!

OLDBOURNE. Harry! please! not again! – remember your doctor's advice. Unless you give up insulting the British Broadcasting Corporation, he will not answer for the state of your health.

PETRIE. Leave me alone! I can't resist it. I'm carried away by the thought of those infantile, nepotic liars, time-serving good taste with as much slobber as a savage his totem or fetish. They are a tumour on the life of the nation, with their intolerable middleness; mediocre, so-so, medium, second-

rate; neither fish nor fowl; flat, stale and unprofitable;
depressing to the acute and the dull, at loggerheads with
lack-wits and men of learning, with shining lights and
crack-brains. Not pleasing the one or the other. Cricket-
playing, doctrinaire, accepting; stupid, arid, Christians,
running mad, amok, berserk, doting, frantic with taste,
befooled, infatuate with delicacy and middle-of-the-road
decorum. They please no party, faction, side, class, set or
crowd, except their own sacred band of jumped-up fairy-
godmothers.

OLDBOURNE. You mustn't be so angry, Harry. You're not a
young man anymore.

PETRIE. I can't help it! I can't! Is rage the prerogative of
youth? Must we cool with the years and die when our blood
has chilled to the temperature of the society around us?
Should we tolerate gradual freezing of our anger, watch
bitterness and pain drugged into insensibility? Is anger so
rare a specific that only the young must have access to it?
(*Pause.*) No! We must hurt the feelings of our enemies,
infuriate those we dislike, and never cease to delight in
bringing the hornet's nest about our ears!

Silence.

MADGE. You'll be an asset at the wedding.

QUEENIE. Does it take long to learn the trade?

OLDBOURNE. It depends on the type of person.

GLADYS. My niece, Sandra, is still looking for a job. I
wonder if she'd be interested.

MADGE. She couldn't do better than come to the wedding.
I'm sure Dr Petrie and Miss Oldbourne wouldn't mind.

PETRIE. Not at all. We believe individuals should fulfil
themselves as completely as possible.

The SMALL PART PLAYER *brings on a soapbox upon
which* PETRIE *stands.*

Work, since it occupies so much of one's time, should be a
source of pleasure as well as a means of earning a living;

and most human beings are happiest when using their abilities to the full. If a young man or woman can project spleen, ejaculate malice and fling sly barbs of acrimony, wit and gall; if they have the power to envenom the most charitable company, or to poison the atmosphere of a death-bed – then they could not do better for themselves than to join our ranks, take our money and accept *Pox vobiscum* as their motto.

GLADYS. What about college fees?

PETRIE. Scholarships are offered to those applicants possessing real talent in tactlessness, incivility, ill-breeding, blackguardism and back-biting. Full information of the training, and individual guidance, are given in these pamphlets.

MISS OLDBOURNE *distributes pamphlets from her box to the cast.*

OLDBOURNE. If you haven't made up your mind about a career, or know of anyone hesitating, why not come and have a chat with us? It is a really worthwhile job.

PETRIE. And the key word is – WORTHWHIILE.

OLDBOURNE. A job for a lifetime.

PETRIE. No salary limit. You're paid as much as you are worth. The work is judged entirely on results, and it is impossible to hide failure.

OLDBOURNE. Dr Petrie has been in practice for years. He can make a seasoned critic swoon with shame; has, on occasions, insulted the highest in the land. Politicians go in fear of him.

PETRIE. Actresses tremble.

OLDBOURNE. – the clergy mention his name in their prayers.

PETRIE. Boxers blush.

OLDBOURNE. – hostesses lose their heads when he is mentioned.

PETRIE. Poets scream.

OLDBOURNE. – men of the world join the Foreign Legion to
forget.

PETRIE. Miss Oldbourne has bitched her way from Bishop's
Waltham to Biskra, clawed and played the cat up and down
the blue Nile, around the Hellespont, across the Kalahari,
and under the Pacific – fouled Arabia and made her name a
byword among the mujiks. In the clubs and chambers of the
Great World they speak her name in whispers. The Kremlin
and the Vatican agree that Grace Oldbourne is the greatest
living exponent of giving offence where offence is due.

BOTH. Our organisation believes in the efficacy of the insult!

Silence.

MADGE. It sounds a lovely job.

GLADYS. I'll pass the information on to Sandra.

WEBBER. Now, Petrie, how about a final demonstration. Just
to oblige, eh?

PETRIE. Very well.

He fires his pistol.

QUEENIE. Freddy Grisewood.

MADGE. Lady Barnet.

GLADYS. Noël Coward.

SYKES. Richard Dimbleby.

WEBBER. Gaitskell.

FRED. Macmillan.

Silence.

PETRIE. You've set me a difficult task. These are figures
hopelessly beyond the range of insult. You can't apply
ordinary standards to – say Grisewood: one would take him
to be a symbol, some kind of Portland Place myth of the
ideal man, if his own particular brand of thick-witted drivel
were not unique. – Lady Barnet, a harmless, non habit-
forming narcotic. Coward, an almost perfect example of

the unnatural idiot. – Dimbleby, a fat, ugly, royalist martyr. Gaitskell, a seedy, politically leprous, broken-winded, moribund ex-radical, infecting his party with galloping consumption. Or MACMILLAN! – a professional zombie leading us into the valley of the shadow.

Silence. MISS OLDBOURNE *stares at him.*

OLDBOURNE (*incredulous*). Harry! you're a genius. You've insulted the insult-proof.

Wild cheers, both on and offstage. PETRIE *is lifted shoulder high and carried out. Silence. Blackout. Light up on* FRED.

FRED. Joe Muggins has to clear up, as usual.

He removes the soapbox, brings on and sets up a pair of French windows. They are not connected to flats and no attempt must be made to conceal the brace.

Silence. Enter the OLD MAN.

FRED. How's life treating you, Dad? Feeling better?

OLD MAN. I'm about the same.

FRED. About the same?

OLD MAN. About the same, yes. (*Pause.*) You've heard Queenie's talking of living her own life. At thirty-four. It's no age, is it?

FRED. Not at all.

Silence.

OLD MAN. The roses I planted have turned out to be duds.

FRED. Have you tried making a complaint?

OLD MAN. I think I will. (*Pause.*) We were so keen on having them. They were company in the long evenings.

FRED. It's a lot of trouble rearing them. The thing is (I may be barking up the wrong tree) – the basic fault is, that they're conventional at heart; they want a settled life, you see. And you can't give it to them.

OLD MAN. Do you think I'm doing wrong?

FRED. You ought to have made enquiries before you took them on.

OLD MAN (*angrily*). What help is it to say that? (*Pause.*) It's not just the roses, you know? It's everything in the garden; not a green shoot in sight. Queenie's refused to have anything to do with me. That hasn't helped.

FRED. You are in the wars.

OLD MAN. I don't know what to do for the best.

FRED. Why not hire. The Plant Hire Service is supposed to be good. You can get anything from a geranium to a cricket lawn. You pay a few bob each week.

OLD MAN. I wouldn't dare. If I hired a garden and I spoiled it – it doesn't bear thinking about.

FRED. Why don't you go in for these moods they're advertising? I'm sure you'd get on better with them.

OLD MAN. I want to avoid creating an atmosphere.

FRED. – Sorrow and Anger (that's a good combination) or why not plain Hope? I don't like it myself. A bit too –

OLD MAN. – high?

FRED. Yes. You can't go wrong, they're guaranteed. If any variety fails to please, the shops are authorised to refund full purchase price. You can't be fairer than that.

OLD MAN. They don't suit every taste. Her sister was very queer after taking Zeal last week; and Mrs Pickersgill's become addicted to Optimism.

FRED. That's the way it goes. I'll say one thing, they make a nice change. We had Disappointment and Rage for Christmas. It was a treat really. Susan's on at me to try Despair – but I don't fancy it.

OLD MAN. I wouldn't take to Despair myself.

FRED. She swears by it. They have it every Monday morning regular.

OLD MAN. I'll give it a try.

FRED. The Royal Family are fond of Banality, though it has a funny effect on me. When they're up to their eyes in Banality at some banquet I'm at home with Apathy, Agony, Anguish, Gloom and Heartache.

OLD MAN. They have a better head for it than you.

FRED. Ecstasy is good.

OLD MAN. Not at my age.

FRED. Or Bliss?

OLD MAN. There's not much difference.

FRED. Try a mixture of Verve, Gusto and Fanaticism.

OLD MAN. Are you trying to do me in? At my time of life Patience is the only one I'd dare to trust; Patience with a dash of Apprehension.

Enter QUEENIE.

QUEENIE. What are you doing here?

FRED. I've an hour or two to spare.

QUEENIE. You're invited to tea, don't forget.

OLD MAN. Why didn't Madge tell him herself?

QUEENIE. I'm not speaking to you. If everybody had their deserts you'd be in prison by now – making the garden look a mess. It's spreading, you know that, don't you? You'll have to be put in some kind of an institution if you carry on like this.

OLD MAN. It's nothing to do with me.

QUEENIE. Oh yes it has. You've been up to something silly. The park looks like the Sahara. I don't know what the council will say when they find out. They'll lock you up.

OLD MAN (*going off*). I'd better see if there's anything I can do.

QUEENIE. Leave it alone. Madge wants you. It'll be teatime

soon and who's going to pour the tea?

OLD MAN. Winifred and Mary. It's not a butler's job.

QUEENIE. Winifred and Mary don't exist, as you know quite
well. Off you go and don't let's have any more argument.
(*Exit* OLD MAN.) You'd better go too, Fred.

Exit FRED. *Enter* GLADYS.

GLADYS. I thought they'd be here all day.

QUEENIE. Been waiting long?

GLADYS. About five minutes.

QUEENIE. Well?

GLADYS. Well, what?

QUEENIE. How did the interview go?

GLADYS. I got the job.

QUEENIE. Oh, good! I *am* glad.

GLADYS. I'm a bit nervous.

QUEENIE. Who did you see?

GLADYS. Old Sakyamuni.

QUEENIE. He's the chief eunuch.

GLADYS (*dreamily*). He has lovely ways.

QUEENIE. You'll have to be careful when we get out there;
some of these eunuchs aren't all they seem. (*Pause*.) Did he
give you your grading?

GLADYS. A1 plus.

QUEENIE. That's the highest. You'll be in attendance on
Ramakrishna in person.

GLADYS. Aren't we all?

QUEENIE. Good God, no! Some of the concubines he
inherited from his grandfather. He can't get rid of them,
it wouldn't be right. On the other hand he can't use them.

So he generally gives them away to visiting royalty.

GLADYS. The old chap mentioned that the Mistress of the Robes had committed suttee – so her job's vacant.

QUEENIE. I wonder if Madge –

GLADYS. Why not ask?

QUEENIE. I will, when I get the chance. (*Pause.*) Those pale hands of yours will come in useful at last.

GLADYS. I'm glad I hung on to them.

QUEENIE. I'll take you with me to Madam Sarasvati next time I go – you'll soon get the hang of dancing with a jewel in your navel, and a yashmak should present no special problem. As you pass the upstairs loo, take a peep at the cobras; get used to the idea. We're trying to persuade the Zoo to lend us an elephant for an hour or so; you've no idea of the bother involved!

GLADYS. I'm still dazed by my good fortune.

Exit.

Blackout.

Lights up. PETRIE, OLDBOURNE *and* MADGE *are entering by the windows.*

PETRIE. Oh, dear! I've insulted you again; force of habit, I'm afraid.

MADGE. All work and no play, Dr Petrie.

OLDBOURNE. Do try to relax, Harry.

PETRIE. I am a bit of a nuisance.

MADGE. I've been looking up all your cases. You did cause the riot at the Guildhall luncheon?

OLDBOURNE. We've been resting on our laurels since then.

PETRIE. That's nothing to what's yet to be done – we've managed to wangle an invitation to the Opening of Parliament.

MADGE. You're surely never going to give offence to millions?

OLDBOURNE. It's our secret ambition.

MADGE. Well, I wish you the best of luck.

The OLD MAN *enters carrying a silver teapot, and the* SMALL PART PLAYER *wheels on a tea-trolley. The butler pours, the footman serves.*

MADGE (*in a conversational tone*). After tea I'll get Jimmy to show you the sights – the source of all his wealth, the pedigree mice and his father's Toc-H badge, and there are one or two fine optical illusions to be seen from the end of the road – and perhaps we shall have time to drive out to St Mary's where my daughter Janice went to College.

Enter WEBBER.

WEBBER. There's a pretty kettle of fish outside on the porch. It's been waiting for two hours.

MADGE (*gaily*). More presents! I'll get Ronald to bring them in. (*Calls.*) Ronald! would you see to that?

SPP. Yes, madam. (*Exit.*)

OLDBOURNE. What a lot of gorgeous presents you have; I was admiring them before lunch.

MADGE. I am lucky.

OLDBOURNE. Harry and I are giving you an eye-opener and a well-stretched point.

MADGE (*embarrassed*). You shouldn't really. (*To* WEBBER.) Your sister's gift arrived by the afternoon post.

WEBBER. Really?

MADGE. A doornail (in extremis). However did she think of that? Did you tell her?

WEBBER. I did drop a hint.

MADGE. I hope you were tactful. Fanny has promised a lovely collection of P's and Q's; so we shan't have to buy any for ages.

OLDBOURNE. I must see them.

MADGE. Wilkins, would you bring the presents in here, please?

OLD MAN. Very good, madam. (*Exit.*)

MADGE. Did the car meet you, Jimmy?

WEBBER. It was such a lovely day I thought I'd walk.

MADGE. You pet! to walk! Isn't that original, Dr Petrie?

PETRIE. I don't know how you think of such things.

Enter the OLD MAN *wheeling on the wedding presents.*

MADGE (*getting up*). Now let me see, which shall I show you first. Here's a pair of glasses for seeing the better side of people –

OLDBOURNE. There'll be fights over who's to use them.

WEBBER. Who sent them, dear?

MADGE. Your mother. Actually they're for me. She's given you an Oedipus complex, and that ought to be enough. (*Lifting the presents.*) A roll of haywire, an old wife's tail, a potted itching palm, a duck's arse, and grandstand tickets for the rat race – they'll come in useful. Are we entering by the way?

WEBBER. Wait and see.

OLDBOURNE. A long felt want.

MADGE. As a matter of fact, it's a plastic want. There was no label so I'm not sure who it came from.

PETRIE (*opening a jewel case*). A narrow squeak, and a tight fix –

MADGE *(to* WEBBER). From Len and Peggy. I've tried the fix on, and I think it's going to be far *too* tight. A book of inside leg measurements. (*Opening it.*) Look at that one! Forty-five inches!

OLDBOURNE. He must have a fine long leg.

PETRIE. It will make a pleasant bedside book.

MADGE. And Milly has given me what for; isn't that just like her? She always was mean. (*Pausing to look at another gift.*) What a fantastic present to receive – a milk-jug and sugar basin!

WEBBER. Who sent that?

MADGE. Uncle Bob.

WEBBER. I might have known.

Enter FRED.

FRED. Can I come in?

MADGE. There's always room for one more. Dr Petrie, Miss Oldbourne – my former husband.

FRED.
PETRIE.   } How do you do.
OLDBOURNE.

FRED. Are we any of us old enough to remember the good old days?

PETRIE. They were before my time.

WEBBER. If we none of us can recall them we must talk about them.

OLDBOURNE. Don't talk to me about the old days. If only we had them back again.

FRED. Do you remember –

OLDBOURNE. Shall I ever forget?

FRED. Do you remember the picnic?

PETRIE. What a summer –

OLDBOURNE. What an idyll –

WEBBER. If only we had the old days back again.

OLDBOURNE. When mother was alive –

MADGE. Very much alive –

FRED. Before the war –

MADGE. Before we lost our money –

PETRIE. Before father and mother died.

OLDBOURNE. What I always wanted to know *was* what did Bertie tell you that day on the picnic by the river?

PETRIE. Ah, that picnic by the river –

MADGE. – and poor, poor Bertie.

OLDBOURNE. Now what I always wanted to know *was* what did poor Father have to say when you –

MADGE. – by the river in the sun. We were so happy in the old days.

WEBBER. Before the war.

FRED. Before father and mother died –

OLDBOURNE. And we lost our money and the climate changed so unaccountably for the worst.

PETRIE. Ah, those were the days.

WEBBER. Ah.

MADGE. – now we are old –

FRED. – old –

MADGE. – and we have no money.

WEBBER. In the old days.

MADGE. Very much in the old days.

FRED. – before the –

MADGE. – and the –

WEBBER. – and –

OLDBOURNE. Do you remember the swans by the river?

PETRIE. Do you remember how Bertie fed them with a piece of cake from the hamper?

WEBBER. Do you remember how –

MADGE. – and do you remember when?

OLDBOURNE. What I always wanted to know *was* what did you say to make poor, poor Daisy cry so – that day, by the river, in the sun, so, so, long ago?

Silence.

MADGE (*with relief*). We managed that very nicely, I thought.

FRED. Do you remember how –

MADGE. Now, Fred, you can have too much of a good thing!

OLDBOURNE. Is there anything we've forgotten?

MADGE. Let me see, Picnics, Sunlight, the River, Father and Mother, Before the War, Losing Our Money– Oh! we've forgotten the cost of living.

PETRIE. Growing old is the cost of living.

MADGE. We might stretch a point.

WEBBER. We should have mentioned Morals: the Deterioration of.

FRED. And Modern Youth.

WEBBER. I think we ought to have a go at Modern Youth.

MADGE. What do you think, Dr Petrie?

PETRIE (*looking at his watch*). We'll just about make it I'd say.

MADGE. Who shall it be then?

FRED. I rather like Brian. We do that quite well.

MADGE. You begin Dr Petrie. I always think the first line needs weight.

PETRIE *clears his throat.*

PETRIE. Let us play a game of cricket on the sands, with

Brian.

MADGE. Brian doesn't want to play.

OLDBOURNE. How odd.

WEBBER. How very odd of Brian.

OLDBOURNE. Brian *is* odd, though. Or haven't you noticed how very odd Brian is?

PETRIE. Brian parts his hair on the opposite side to you and I.

FRED. Oh, there's something queer about Brian.

MADGE. Where did he get those shoes?

WEBBER. And he wears shirts marked 'non iron'.

FRED. Oh, there's something queer about Brian.

OLDBOURNE. Have you noticed how, when Brian comes in to tea, he gives a little cough before entering the room? Have you?

WEBBER. Extraordinary!

PETRIE. And he hates organised games –

MADGE. – does Brian.

PETRIE. And double-barrelled names –

MADGE. – does Brian.

WEBBER. It's a shame about Brian.

OLDBOURNE. He goes on marches and things of that sort which I and mother and father and aunt Ellen (who is most awfully good about simply everything) and gran and Bella's friend called Nancy or Myra or Elizabeth and that wonderful woman we met on holiday last year who ran a chicken farm or something – don't understand.

PETRIE. – and he PROTESTS.

MADGE. – does Brian.

WEBBER. It's a dreadful shame about Brian.

OLDBOURNE. Because his family are quite nice really. Well,

there's his sister who's a bit of a bore but quite nice really. Underneath. I mean you can see she's quite nice really. And his mother is really nice. And so is his brother Tom who is married and has a Ford car and three really nice children. And I've never actually met his father but I believe he's quite nice. In fact they all are. Except Brian.

WEBBER. Except Brian.

OLDBOURNE. Brian wears jeans. No. I don't mean on holidays or at weekends or messing about in boats or in the country, where everyone does anyway. No he wears them for weddings and funerals and Christenings and for his sister's twenty-first – and to visit the Frobishers.

ALL. To visit the FROBISHERS!

FRED. Oh, there's definitely something queer about Brian.

Silence.

MADGE. I don't think anybody could grumble at that, could they?

PETRIE. It's hardly Modern Youth, is it?

MADGE. Isn't it?

PETRIE. I'd say it was the attitude of the rebellee to the rebel – I mean, clearly Brian is a bit of a rebel, isn't he?

MADGE. Well, we've always called it Modern Youth, Dr Petrie, and I think it'd better stay that way, if you don't mind.

Enter the OLD MAN.

OLD MAN. Dinner is served, Madam.

MADGE. Thank you, Wilkins.

The OLD MAN *exits.*

MADGE. Do you mind if I go in with Dr Petrie, Grace?

OLDBOURNE. Not at all.

MADGE. – because I want to ask him how to make a spectacle of myself; I've been meaning to try for ages.

All exit, except for FRED. *He comes to the edge of the stage.*

FRED. We're having a night out, Sykes, are you coming?

SYKES. I don't think so.

FRED. Come on, it's in a good cause. We're going to laugh at some of the new buildings. Queenie did a lot of damage in the city over the weekend.

SYKES. Oh, very well.

FRED. Don't breathe a word to Webber; he's fond of the modern scene.

SYKES *goes back to his seat.* QUEENIE *and* GLADYS *cross the stage.*

QUEENIE. He's put the whole thing in reverse, Glad, and he doesn't seem to know how.

GLADYS. You did go on at him.

QUEENIE. He has no sense of proportion: one minute the place is a desert, the next you have to cut your way through the trees in Wigmore Street.

GLADYS. Is it as bad as that?

QUEENIE. It couldn't be worse. Hampstead Heath has joined up with Regent's Park around Euston – they're using porters as beaters to find the platforms at King's Cross, and the new road improvements are ruined at Hyde Park, and they're getting up a grouse shoot in Old Compton Street.

GLADYS. Something ought to be done.

QUEENIE. The Forestry Commission have been round, but he doesn't understand how it came to happen. And the inconvenience he's causing; Harrods are in the middle of a woodland glade.

GLADYS. What with your father spreading the public parks and gardens and Fred organising outings to destroy the buildings, we'll all have to emigrate before long.

Exit.

Lights up on MADGE *and* FRED. *The light coming through the window has a greenish tinge.*

FRED. Look at it out there – like the Everglades!

MADGE. I feel so guilty. (*Pause.*) They're sending Dad to the Middle East to see what he can do for the Arabs. And Queenie's off to India after the wedding. (*Pause.*) I've half-promised to go with her.

FRED. You'd never stand the heat.

MADGE. I could take over the Mistress of the Robes' job.

FRED. It wants a lot of thinking about.

MADGE. Yes.

FRED. Have you considered the drawbacks?

MADGE. No, I'm leaving the drawbacks till we get out there and then I can consider them at my leisure.

FRED. There's the banshees.

MADGE. Oh, dear!

FRED. – and the ghouls.

MADGE. I can take care of myself. Living's impossible over here.

FRED. It is anywhere.

MADGE. It'll be a new life.

FRED. It won't be such a new life; it'll be the old dog-eared, shop-soiled life in a new country. (*Pause.*) You haven't taken the shape of the buildings into consideration, have you?

MADGE. I'll get used to them.

FRED. It's easy to say that. You haven't lived with buildings of a different shape. You're used to our shapes.

MADGE. It'll make a change.

FRED. You're not prepared for the worst, are you?

MADGE. I'm looking forward to it.

FRED. And turbans. They'll worry the life out of you.

MADGE. All I have to do is – keep calm.

FRED. How are you going to put up with sacred cows, and begging friars, and dervishes, and ruling castes; and are you prepared to bow to the Buddha's tooth? I daresay you would be. (*Pause*.) They'll never stand for you washing so much.

MADGE. Queenie told me not to worry.

FRED. I can't picture you in a howdah. It won't agree with you. And how will you cope with a teffinah or caftan?

MADGE. You don't understand. I'll be the Mistress of the Robes – it's only Gladys that's going into the harem.

FRED. It'll sap your vitality. (*Pause*.) The barbaric splendour –

MADGE. – the exotic east –

FRED. – the outposts of the Empire –

MADGE. – those nights by the Ganges.

FRED. The swaying palms and the camels and the seductive dances of the Murri-murri, oh I can see it all!

MADGE. I feel as though I'm in a different world.

FRED. – cities of intrigue.

MADGE. – veiled beauties.

FRED. There's no getting away from it, the world's a strange place.

MADGE. You can't deny it.

FRED. The Orient is beckoning –

MADGE. – it's calling me –

FRED. – the spice trade –

MADGE. The East India Company –

FRED. And how will you go on if they decide to have a durbah? And Calcutta, mistress of the East –

MADGE (*carried away*). Mistress of the East –

FRED. It's close in the summer.

MADGE. We'll be in the hills; above the Eternal Snows.

FRED. And the population problem. And the yaks and the burning ghats, and the ivory and pigeon's blood rubies –

MADGE. – and the dawn coming up like thunder –

FRED. – sepoys –

MADGE. – flying fish –

FRED. – curry –

MADGE. – Poona –

FRED. – North of Katmandu –

MADGE. – tea –

FRED. – gurkhas –

MADGE. – thuggee –

FRED. – land of mystery –

MADGE. – soma –

FRED. – purdah –

BOTH. – MOTHER INDIA!

Silence.

MADGE. How did we come to lose it?

FRED. That Lord Beaverbrook had a hand in it; he's too fond of throwing away the Empire. Too cavalier by half.

MADGE. He wants us to give Gibraltar to the Spaniards.

FRED. – and Malta to the Italians.

MADGE. – and Hong Kong to the Chinese.

FRED. – and the six counties to the Irish. (*Pause.*) I read between the lines in that paper of his – I know who lost us India.

MADGE. We should have been firm.

FRED. Showed no nonsense.

MADGE. Shot the lot of them.

FRED. I knew you were reactionary at heart, dear.

Silence. Enter PETRIE, OLDBOURNE, SYKES, *and* QUEENIE.

QUEENIE. It's taken us the best part of half-an-hour getting through the primulas.

MADGE. I only planted them last week.

PETRIE. Are we all prepared?

QUEENIE. We'd better go the front way.

MADGE. I can't face the ivy – it's getting beyond a joke. We'll go through the French windows and risk it.

QUEENIE. I thought he was going to get a flame-thrower?

MADGE. It's still on order.

Exit.

The stage is in darkness. Sounds of laughter. The crash of falling masonry and breaking glass.

Lights up. All re-enter.

QUEENIE (*breathless*). I'm worn out.

MADGE. I bet you are. You should have left the Festival Hall alone.

QUEENIE. I couldn't resist all the glass. Oh, dear! I shall have to sit down.

MADGE. Bitten off more than you can chew, haven't you?

QUEENIE. Just let me get my breath back.

FRED. Are you game for the Daily Mirror building, Dr Petrie?

PETRIE. Certainly.

FRED. And you, Grace?

OLDBOURNE. It'll have to be moral support, I'm afraid.

FRED. We'd better call it a day after this. What do you think, Sykes?

SYKES. Yes. We've done enough damage for one night.

QUEENIE. Wait for me. I can't start yet.

PETRIE. Couldn't we have the reactions while we recover our breath? I'm sure we're all interested to know what the authorities have to say.

FRED. We can't have reactions before the event.

QUEENIE. Reactions first, events afterwards.

MADGE. It isn't logic.

PETRIE. Who cares about logic; I don't.

MADGE. Oh, very well.

Enter the SMALL PART PLAYER.

SPP. Official reaction to the disturbing news of yesterday's protest-laughter is one of deep shock. The Prime Minister said 'We must take strong measures in order to combat the coming crisis.'

PETRIE. And what are these 'strong measures'?

SPP. The Government are seriously contemplating the setting up of a committee to investigate the cause and progress of laughter. A satisfactory solution to the problem, it is sincerely hoped, is on the way.

PETRIE. And meanwhile what do the Government propose to do?

SPP. It is not considered a serious enough problem to warrant any direct interference. The Prime Minister is flying to Washington to consult with the President.

PETRIE. Good.

SPP. The Queen is flying to Rome to visit the Pope.

PETRIE. Excellent.

SPP. The Pope has called upon Catholics everywhere to pray
    for the triumph of Christian thinking.

PETRIE. Splendid.

SPP. The Foreign Secretary is visiting Spain and Portugal; it is
    hoped this will bring about a closer understanding between
    the democracies.

PETRIE. Admirable.

SPP. The Leader of the Opposition has expressed alarm.

PETRIE. And what are the Opposition doing about the
    situation?

SPP. Why nothing, what would you have them do? The Leader
    of the Opposition has expressed his alarm; that is enough.
    He is in complete agreement with the Prime Minister: the
    matter is not serious, it must never be allowed to assume the
    proportions of a major crisis.

PETRIE. But with no buildings, and the forests growing larger
    each day, it *is* a major crisis.

SPP. Official sources state that if we keep perfectly calm, and
    perfectly still, it will go away.

PETRIE. Thank you.

    Exit the SMALL PART PLAYER.

OLDBOURNE. Are we all ready?

MADGE. What's the order?

FRED. Dr Petrie first. Queenie – are you ready?

QUEENIE. Yes.

FRED. Dr Petrie will aim at the foundations, Sykes a little
    higher? Queenie and Madge are concentrating on the
    windows as usual, and Grace – is it OK if we leave the
    girders to you?

OLDBOURNE. Quite all right, quite all right.

FRED. Good. Then, off we go.

He conducts the laughter varying from bass to treble. The building is imagined out front. With each laugh or series of laughs the sound of falling masonry and cracking glass increases.

PETRIE. What a hideous shape. (*Laughs.*)

MADGE. I don't like all that red. (*Laughs.*)

OLDBOURNE. Acres of glass and concrete – how horrible. (*Laughs.*)

SYKES. Fancy those readers subscribing to erect such an eyesore. (*Laughs.*)

QUEENIE. I wouldn't work there. (*Laughs.*)

MADGE. It gives me the horrors. (*Laughs.*)

The laughter grows more and more hysterical while FRED *conducts furiously, bringing up each solo, duet, trio or quartette with considerable skill.*

PETRIE. – glass.
OLDBOURNE. – concrete.
MADGE. – red paint.
PETRIE. – glorious idiocy.
OLDBOURNE. – visible for mile upon mile.

SYKES. – awful.
QUEENIE. – rubbishy modern filth; better a bomb site than THAT!
SYKES. – it hurts my eyes.
QUEENIE. – ugh!

SYKES. – of no architectural interest.
PETRIE. – none whatever.
SYKES. – worthless.
PETRIE. – sterile, dirty slop, recrement, feculence, sewer; glass-rookery, a glass ant-hill, a glass fester, frotting, rotting, concrete verbosity, a monument to a desert, to a vacuum, to a wilderness, a glass and concrete pustule!

SYKES. I execrate.

MADGE. – beshrew –

OLDBOURNE. – denounce –

PETRIE. – curse uphill and down dale the architectural
wonders of the age!

Enter WEBBER.

WEBBER. Stop it! Stop this puerile display at once!

MADGE. Oh, hallo, Jimmy. I didn't know you were coming.

WEBBER. So you are responsible?

MADGE. I said I'd help Fred. He organised the outing.

PETRIE. And very successful it's been. Most of the contemporary scene – Gone!

OLDBOURNE. – wrecked.

FRED. – in ruins.

QUEENIE. – razed to the ground.

SYKES. – mounds of rubble.

MADGE (*throwing her arms around* WEBBER*'s neck*). Con-
gratulate us! We've done such a lot of wanton destruction.

WEBBER. It is a very dangerous ability you have discovered
in yourselves. It should be used for the good of the community, not employed for pleasure. Do you want to ruin society
and civilisation with your laughter?

MADGE. Yes, oh yes!

WEBBER. I shall have to think this over very seriously. I'll
see you in the morning. My attitude towards you, and the
prospect of a happy life together has changed materially.

Exit.

FRED. Now, just once more should do it. And then we'll call
it a day.

Laughter and more crashes as darkness falls.

ACT THREE

FRED *enters and brings on the chairs and standard lamp.*
QUEENIE *sits watching.*

House lights fade. Enter MADGE.

MADGE. Where's Dad?

QUEENIE. Do you want him?

MADGE. No.

QUEENIE. He's packing.

MADGE. Packing?

QUEENIE. They're fetching him after the ceremony.

MADGE. He has to make a show of himself.

QUEENIE. He can't go by the road – oh! you don't know?

MADGE. Know?

QUEENIE. Look! (*She points out of the windows.*)

MADGE. Who did that?

QUEENIE. It's those runner beans – I said you shouldn't have
planted them with him as he is.

MADGE. How are we ever going to get to church?

QUEENIE. I asked the vicar to come here. Grace has gone to
fetch him. I told her to notch each beanstalk as she passed.

MADGE (*sitting down*). I'm so depressed.

QUEENIE. It is depressing.

MADGE. We shan't be able to stay here. Life isn't worth
living if you have to go on safari for groceries.

QUEENIE. Things are never as bad as they seem. Look on the
bright side. (*Pause.*) I hope Grace won't insult the vicar
before she gets him into the forest.

MADGE. Does it matter.

QUEENIE. He'll take offence and get away.

MADGE. It all seems so difficult! (*Bursts into tears.*)

FRED. See what you've done?

QUEENIE. You're no help. Standing there without opening your mouth.

FRED. I had nothing to say.

SYKES *enters.*

SYKES. Hallo.

FRED. Hallo.

SYKES. I'm drunk.

FRED. That's no news; Queen Anne's dead.

SYKES. I got rid of my old values last night.

MADGE. That's a silly thing to do.

QUEENIE. You'll regret it.

MADGE. You ought to have kept some of them.

SYKES. None. Not a single one. How can I own permanent values?

MADGE. Values do deteriorate fast.

QUEENIE. Old-fashioned values are no use.

SYKES. And attitudes are the same.

MADGE. Wally and Joan had a lovely wartime attitude – what use is it now?

QUEENIE. None.

FRED. Look at Wally's father, his attitude hasn't changed since nineteen thirty-nine.

MADGE. He looks such a fool on Sundays.

FRED. He's a stubborn man.

MADGE. Wilful.

QUEENIE. Nothing makes a man so ridiculous as an old-fashioned attitude.

FRED (*prompting* SYKES). Go on. – the respectable members of society –

MADGE (*settling back in her chair*). This is the very latest in attitudes, but I don't think it's going to catch on.

QUEENIE. You do it so well.

MADGE. – the respectable members of society are –

SYKES. Perverts.

MADGE. Perverts! What a lyrical concept!

QUEENIE. Go on, go on! Why do you keep interrupting him in the middle of what he is saying.

SYKES. The most respectable are the most perverty.

FRED. Take Webber.

MADGE. Or Mrs Dale –

SYKES. – she sounds the biggest old prude unhung, but I'll bet she thinks of sex twenty-four hours a day. All the time she's talking to her mother or to Isabel, I'll bet she's nearly going out of her mind thinking of sex.

MADGE. Definitely.

QUEENIE. She'd never admit it.

MADGE. She's a modest woman.

QUEENIE. I'd be surprised if her attitudes weren't up-to-date in the right places.

FRED. It must get her down.

QUEENIE. The tantalising life she leads.

MADGE. She has lovely ways with her.

QUEENIE. Never a word or a gesture out of place.

FRED. She's a phenomenon of the age.

MADGE. Definitely.

QUEENIE. And she'd be the first to admit it.

SYKES. I must keep on, on and on, every syllable is a new attitude forming.

QUEENIE. I think you might have warned us.

SYKES. Warned you?

QUEENIE. Coming here without an attitude and then expecting us to sit by while you make yourself another.

MADGE. You're too sensitive, Queenie.

QUEENIE. I'm going. I can't be bothered watching.

MADGE. No. Wait.

SYKES. . . . what's the difference between living off the earnings of one woman, or off hundreds of women in a factory. There are just pimps and super-pimps.

Silence.

MADGE. I don't like that attitude. (*Pause.*) It's in advance of avant-garde. (*Pause.*) Don't you think so!

FRED. It's a bit rum.

QUEENIE. I suppose he'd better go through with it, though where it's going to lead is anybody's guess. Go on. You can't leave it unfinished. Half an attitude is worse than none.

SYKES. That's all, I'm afraid. (*Pause.*) I'll go now, don't mind me any more.

QUEENIE. Well –

MADGE. – are you sure –

FRED. – are you sure you'll be safe?

SYKES. Quite sure.

MADGE. You must get a better attitude than that.

SYKES. I'll be OK. (*Pause.*) Goodbye, then. I'll see you before you go.

MADGE. Cheerio.

Exit SYKES.

FRED. He's a funny chap.

MADGE. Everyone's entitled to their opinions.

QUEENIE (*pause*). Jimmy sent you a note.

MADGE. When?

QUEENIE. Earlier on.

MADGE. Where is it?

QUEENIE. I don't know.

The OLD MAN *enters. He has on a pair of dark glasses and a white suit and solar topee.*

MADGE. Wilkins, isn't there a note for me?

OLD MAN. I believe it was put on the hall table, Madam.

MADGE. I'd like to see it.

OLD MAN. Very well, Madam.

Exit.

MADGE. What's he got up in that outfit for? Enough to frighten the crows.

QUEENIE. He's leaving for Damascus after the wedding.

MADGE. A fine thing when he has to make a laughing stock of himself at his age.

Enter the OLD MAN *with a note on a tray.*

MADGE. Thank you, Wilkins.

OLD MAN. The guests have arrived, Madam. Quite a number are in the garden. The lengthening shadows are keeping them amused. All our best wishes, Madam.

MADGE. Thank you, Wilkins.

Exit the OLD MAN. MISS OLDBOURNE *rushes through the windows.*

OLDBOURNE. Is he here?

MADGE. Who?

OLDBOURNE. The vicar.

MADGE. Should he be?

OLDBOURNE. I've lost him! Oh, dear, can you ever forgive me?

MADGE. You've lost him?

OLDBOURNE. I was very careful. I notched each beanstalk. I told him to keep close to me. When we got him into the forest, I relaxed a little and tried a mild insult or two. His reactions were unpredictable! He ran away. I thought he'd be here.

MADGE. We'd better send out search parties.

OLDBOURNE. Would you come and help, Queenie?

QUEENIE. If you want.

OLDBOURNE. You'd better stay and see to your guests. Oh, dear! What a thing to happen.

QUEENIE. If he's lost among the polyanthus we're wasting our time.

Exit OLDBOURNE *and* QUEENIE.

MADGE. I wouldn't have such a thing happen to a clergyman, it isn't right.

FRED. A prayer or two works wonders.

MADGE. Now, Fred! Don't blaspheme. I'm not what you'd call religious, but I do like to show respect. I will say one thing for the vicar, he did know when to kneel and when to stand. It's not easy.

FRED. It isn't.

MADGE. I went with Janice to St Christopher's last week, and we got everything wrong. She didn't know when to kneel and when to sit.

FRED. And you feel so *public*, sitting there alone.

MADGE. You do. Mind you, the vicar was very nice. He invited us backstage to his dressing-room afterwards, said he was sorry there wasn't more of an audience.

FRED. It must be disheartening.

MADGE. 'Well, vicar,' I said, 'it's no good blaming the critics if you're getting empty houses.'

FRED. Even allowing for the popularity of farce it's been a long run.

MADGE. Exactly. After two thousand years they must have recovered production costs.

FRED. I'd say so.

MADGE. The vicar is all for a good press agent, a better business manager, and a new producer. But I said, 'Vicar, you'll never have any luck unless you change your star.'

FRED. He's past it.

MADGE. I've never been keen on him.

FRED. He's over-publicised.

MADGE. So the vicar admitted that in a last resort the management were prepared to get rid of one or two members of the cast.

FRED. It would be a pity if such an old-established firm went out of business.

MADGE. A great pity.

FRED. They never closed, you know? They have been responsible for some of the world's finest spectacles.

MADGE. At prices well within our means.

FRED. The Dark Ages – they started them. Ignorance, Superstition, Barbarism – what a show! Intolerance, Bigotry – I could go on for hours.

MADGE. St Paul! what a comedian.

FRED. And then, there was the burning of the books and works of art, anti-semitism, censorship, and a leader we could all look up to. You'd be surprised how many modern things are copyright.

MADGE. Did you ever see anything to beat the Acts of the Apostles? It was a real hoot.

FRED. The Inquisition ran it close. All those cardinals and Pope Paul III (he was one of those real old-time red-nosed comics, with a special line in off-colour jokes and heresy).

MADGE. What about the Lambeth Palace mob?

FRED. You'll never get a funnier show.

MADGE. This book of theirs is a best-seller, and from the bits I've seen it deserves to be.

FRED. I couldn't help smiling at some of the turns of phrase.

MADGE. Mind you, I don't think the Church ought to take the micky out of the Bible; it isn't right.

The sound of elephants trumpeting.

MADGE. Listen! (*Bugles and the elephants.*) The elephants. Can you hear them?

FRED. They're early.

MADGE. She ordered them for two o'clock.

FRED. What are you going to do if they don't find the vicar?

MADGE. I don't know.

FRED. Let's get up and go.

MADGE. Go? Where? And Jimmy? He'd be so upset if he came and found we'd gone without him.

FRED. You're not going to marry him?

MADGE. Did you think I would?

FRED. Not when I saw that note. He's broken it off, hasn't he?

MADGE. Yes.

FRED. So we're both jilted.

MADGE. Has Susan –

FRED. She told me last night. (*Pause. Sound of elephants.*)
Hark at them. I've always wanted elephants. I never dared
to do anything about it.

MADGE. It's a dangerous obsession.

FRED. I can't break myself of it.

MADGE. Why don't you come with us?

FRED. With you?

MADGE. To India.

FRED. What are you thinking of?

MADGE. You'll be sorry.

FRED. I expect I will.

MADGE. You'll lead a life of regret.

FRED. What a prospect!

MADGE. You'd be so happy looking after the beasts.

FRED. Tigers.

MADGE. Rhinos.

FRED. Crocodiles.

MADGE. And as many snakes as you could count.

FRED. And birds too, I suppose.

MADGE. Peacocks, macaws, widgeons, eagles.

FRED. It's too good to be true.

MADGE. Don't stand there thinking about it.

FRED. I wouldn't have the right boots.

MADGE. No.

FRED. I'd need a different kind of hat.

MADGE. A big, wide, hat.

FRED. A big, flat, hat.

MADGE. – with a brim; so smart.

FRED. I'm afraid I might prove inadequate.

MADGE. Not with a smart hat and a pair of boots – no one
could prove inadequate.

FRED. I'd need a different personality.

MADGE. It's not good for you, all this indecision. It's silly to
say it keeps you from making mistakes, it doesn't. And even
if it did that would be no excuse.

FRED (*pause*). I've been hearing things lately.

MADGE. What kind of things?

FRED. Bells ringing.

MADGE. And what's wrong with that?

FRED. Voices talking.

MADGE. If you don't like them, why do you listen?

FRED. They fascinate me.

MADGE. I think it needs looking into. You ought to see old
Johnson.

FRED. He's dead.

MADGE. When did it happen?

FRED. I don't think he was ever alive.

MADGE. It was that surgery of his.

*Sounds of argument offstage. Exclamations of dismay.
Faint applause.*

FRED. Petrie must have started early.

MADGE. Without the vicar.

Enter the SMALL PART PLAYER *as a guest. He walks
across the stage.*

FRED. Who was that?

MADGE. Some relation of Jimmy's.

FRED. I hope he finds his way through the garden.

MADGE. Yes. (*Pause.*) What do these voices say?

FRED. It's a graveyard.

MADGE. Is that all?

FRED. It's a graveyard, a graveyard.

MADGE. You shouldn't listen. No good will come of it.

FRED. How old are we now?

MADGE. I've lost count. Forty – forty-five.

FRED. We'll die in the end. (*Pause.*) Years we keep hammer-
ing away at it. (*Pause.*) In the end we manage it. (*Pause.*
Sigh.) We'll manage it in the end. It won't be so bad.

MADGE. It's a sad life.

FRED. It's lonely.

MADGE. Yes.

FRED. All those years.

MADGE. All the foreign parts unvisited.

FRED. Lonely. (*Pause.*) All the people that have ever lived . . .
their lives were lonely, they were lonely, miserable, or
happy, and now it's over. (*Pause.*) How long have we been
re-married?

MADGE. We're not married!

FRED. There was a time-lapse.

MADGE. I must have missed it.

The lights dim and the stage is plunged into darkness.

MADGE. No! it's come. There is a time-lapse. You were
premature. I thought I'd missed it.

MADGE *exits.*

Lights up. FRED *is lying on the ground.* MADGE *re-enters.*

Silence. Sound of the elephants.

MADGE. Listen! You'd better go and feed them. It's getting to be a problem.

FRED. The polyanthus are higher –

MADGE. – the marigolds are spreading –

FRED. – the forest has crept up to the house –

MADGE. – the convolvulus climbs in at the window –

FRED. – we lost the dog last week –

MADGE. – strangled by the honeysuckle.

Silence.

FRED. It's six months since the elephants arrived.

MADGE. Queenie's getting impatient. (*Pause.*) What were you doing before I came in?

FRED. I was trying to die.

MADGE. Oh. (*Pause.*) That shouldn't be difficult.

FRED. I was trying to do it without fuss. (*Pause.*) You don't understand, do you? (*Pause.*) I was trying to die without a lot of fuss. I didn't know how.

MADGE. You need a better brain.

FRED. I've never been educated to it.

MADGE. If you'd received an education, I daresay you could have done it.

FRED. I can't do anything.

MADGE. You're a failure.

FRED. What can I do?

MADGE. You can dream.

FRED. It's the only thing, isn't it. (*Pause.*) I'd better go to India with you.

MADGE. You could die.

FRED. I can't. I can't do it.

MADGE. You were doing it a minute ago, before I came in.

FRED. Only in a half-hearted way. I'd just been outside, in the forest; I saw the sun coming down through the leaves; I felt it, warm, silky, upon my neck. I wish I'd never been born, but I don't want to die. (*Pause.*) I can't hate it enough; I can't hate living enough. If I had sufficient hate I could die.

Silence.

Enter the OLD MAN.

OLD MAN. We're waiting to begin. They've found another vicar.

FRED. It's too late. We're going to India to forget our troubles.

OLD MAN. I'm not. Catch me out there with the bleeding sahibs and memsahibs.

MADGE. I'll be getting along.

FRED. Yes.

MADGE. I have to dress for the part.

FRED. All right, dear.

MADGE *exits.*

OLD MAN. So it's over?

FRED. Help me to get these things cleared away. We're packing up.

They remove everything onstage.

OLD MAN. What are we going to do?

FRED. We're giving up. I can't die. I'm a failure. I think I'm a failure. So I'm going on a journey. I know where this journey leads – it's a long journey. Idle dreams. Dreams.

OLD MAN. You needn't tell me. I've been half asleep all my life. (*Elephant noises.*) Listen, just listen. (*Pause.*) Elephants, tethered to the trees in the forest. We'd have to leave anyway – everybody's leaving – the whole country covered in trees. (*Sound of a helicopter*.) There they are, coming to fetch me!

FRED. Flying you out there, aren't they?

OLD MAN. Yes. I can't remember how I did it. I'm worried in case I reverse it again.

FRED. They know what they're doing.

OLD MAN. If I turned the whole of the Middle East into a desert without oases –

FRED. Have a bit of tact.

OLD MAN. It was touch and go whether I accepted.

FRED. Eunice Foster is in business in Damascus.

OLD MAN. I'll have to look her up. She was a nice woman. I never heard anyone say a word against her. Not a word. except the time she bit her old man.

FRED. Bit her old man?

OLD MAN. Bit him one Sunday dinner time.

FRED *has removed the furniture from the stage and dismantled the French windows. He drags on a theatrical hamper and takes out an Indian robe, turban and slippers. He dresses behind the hamper.*

OLD MAN. That's a lovely bit of silk. Is it your going away dress?

FRED. Yes.

OLD MAN. It must have cost a bob or two.

FRED. Her old man paid for it.

OLD MAN. I shall have to get the Sheik to let me have something similar. After all I'll be doing important work.

FRED. No doubt about it.

Silence.

OLD MAN. Why do you suppose she would bite her old man?

FRED. She was unhappy, I suppose. He always did the best for them. All I can think is that as he got older *she* got worse. Maybe because she was so conscious of him growing old.

OLD MAN. So – she can bite him?

FRED. Well, I don't think –

OLD MAN. No. Mind you – between ourselves – strictly for the record – don't breathe a word –

FRED. You know me.

OLD MAN. Not a word to a living soul – there *is* cannibalism in the family. Her uncle (the one with the limp) disappeared sudden. They said he'd gone abroad.

FRED. Go on!

OLD MAN. I'm not kidding. There you are. That's life. Life is what you make it.

FRED. You've got to take the rough with the smooth.

OLD MAN. You never said a truer word.

FRED (*pause*). Does this turban suit me?

OLD MAN. It might have been made for you. (*Pause.*) It came as a big shock when old Webber jilted Madge.

FRED. It's all for the best.

OLD MAN. She doesn't bear him a grudge, though. She's used her influence to get him a job in charge of the eunuchs.

FRED. Good of her really.

OLD MAN. She's got a lovely nature.

FRED (*pushing the hamper into the wings*). You'd better mind out of the way, Dad. The elephants will be here any minute.

Sound of elephants trumpeting and a band playing martial music. Enter QUEENIE *as Maharanee,* GLADYS *as concubine,* MADGE *as Mistress of the Robes, and* WEBBER *as Commander in Chief of the Eunuchs.* SYKES, OLDBOURNE, PETRIE *and the* SMALL PART PLAYER *following. Trumpets. Music. A ship's siren.*

QUEENIE. Here we are – about to embark on a new life, a new beginning. On this foundation a brave future will be built.

MADGE. This is a wonderful dream-fantasy.

QUEENIE. I knew you'd enjoy yourself.

MADGE. Dr Petrie, will you carry on from here? I think we all trust you.

PETRIE. (*standing on his soapbox, which the* SMALL PART PLAYER *brings forward*). Those who are content to be carefree derive the greatest enjoyment from a dream. Unfortunately there are some who are wrapped up in the details of reality, having no time, no joy, of dreaming. (*Pause. He clears his throat.*) We are going to India –

ALL. To India!

PETRIE. We have our valid passports.

MADGE. -- our return transportation tickets, and funds.

QUEENIE. We have our visas.

SYKES. India. We are escaping from the jungle, the undergrowth, the rankness and decay –

WEBBER. – the shrubs –

MADGE. – outsize flowers and monstrous ferns.

OLDBOURNE. We have enquired at our banks for the rate of exchange. The rupee is rising.

MADGE. Rising.

PETRIE. Constantly rising. The elephants are ready. The trumpeters. A new life awaits us in a far country. Accommodation is available to us in the beautiful Palace of the Emperors –

MADGE. – at Sutpura –

QUEENIE. Of which I am Maharanee. (*Pause.*) I love that part. I'm glad we had India.

MADGE. Not Zulus.

FRED. I wanted Zulus.

MADGE. Just because you fancy yourself in feathers is no excuse for becoming a Zulu.

WEBBER. I wanted Mandarins; Sykes wanted White Russia.

MADGE. It's too late now; we had to budget.

PETRIE. We had to budget. Zulus and Mandarins, the Imperial Guard, Satrapies and Empires –

OLDBOURNE. – are expensive.

PETRIE. Incas and Aztecs and pure-blooded Polynesians –

OLDBOURNE. – are expensive.

MADGE. India is well within our means.

Pause.

QUEENIE. What about the language?

WEBBER. Language.

PETRIE. The British today, by and large, are not so language conscious as they once were. We find we can get abroad with the help of a few phrases, words, including the cardinals and ordinals and days of the week.

FRED. The language difficulty mustn't be allowed to hamper a dream.

MADGE. Mustn't be allowed to hamper a fantasy.

Pause.

MADGE. We must remember to be polite.

FRED. It pays to be polite. We shan't call our untouchable servants 'untouchables', we shall call them –

MADGE. – helps –

WEBBER. – angels –

GLADYS. – assistants –

FRED. – reliefs –

OLDBOURNE. – supports –

PETRIE. – this gives us confidence in our authority. We shall have servants.

GLADYS. – and riches –

MADGE. – and beautiful buildings –

WEBBER. – an autocratic madness and, at the same time, a liberal sanity; combining the desired and the to-be-desired; reconciling unreconcilables.

FRED. We shall be the favourites of princes; ride in howdahs and palanquins; live in purple-hued throne rooms; dine off golden platters; listen to the music of flutes; watch the dancing of exotic slaves –

PETRIE. – of either gender.

MADGE. How marvellous!

QUEENIE. Wonderful!

PETRIE. And utterly unlikely. But is that to be despised? We shall not despise the unlikely. It is because we regard the improbable, the incredible and the contrary-to-reason as being of importance that we have made these remarks, here, at the commencement of our journey.

OLDBOURNE. Our long journey –

ALL. To India!

PETRIE. Now, to the more conventional, lifting your glasses for which you have paid sixpence, studying your programme, we shall say Goodbye. We have our guide-books to the myth, our publicity brochures of the symbol, expect moments, expect promise.

OLDBOURNE. The elephants are waiting.

WEBBER. The ships are waiting.

FRED. The tides are waiting.

MADGE. Waiting to take us away. (*Ship's siren.*)

QUEENIE. To a better life.

ALL. TO INDIA!

Lights fade onstage and rise up on the auditorium.

The End.

THE VISITORS

Characters

KEMP
BASSET
MRS PLATT
SISTER MARQUAND
SIMS
O'HARA
BROWN
FAZAKERLEY
CAMERON

ACT ONE

A hospital ward. The bell rings for the beginning of visiting time. Footsteps approach over polished wood floors.

MRS PLATT *detaches herself from the other visitors, and wanders about looking lost. We see her speak to the* SISTER, *who then walks away not taking much notice.*

MRS PLATT *walks across the ward, peering about her short-sightedly. Seeing the person she is looking for, a very old man, she heads in his direction.*

MRS PLATT. Here you are!

KEMP. Oh, here you are.

MRS PLATT. They've moved you then? When did they do that?

KEMP. Yesterday.

MRS PLATT. Why did they do that?

KEMP. What's it like out?

MRS PLATT. The sun's shining.

KEMP. Isn't it raining?

MRS PLATT. Of course it's not raining. On the verandah's where you ought to be – in the fresh air.

KEMP. I shall be there soon enough.

MRS PLATT (*rummaging in a hold-all*). I brought you these. (*Produces a tin of toffee.*) I know you're not supposed to have them, but I thought you'd like to.

KEMP. I don't know.

MRS PLATT. I'll just slip them under your pillow. (*Doing so.*) Something sweet, that's what you need to keep your pecker up.

KEMP. I'd rather have a smoke of my pipe.

MRS PLATT. You know what they said?

KEMP. I'm going anyway.

MRS PLATT. You're not to talk like that! Lovely flowers they have in this ward.

KEMP. Like a funeral.

MRS PLATT. You're in a cheerful mood, I must say.

KEMP. Nothing much to be cheerful about.

MRS PLATT. That isn't the spirit! What did you have for dinner?

KEMP. They daren't give me any.

MRS PLATT. They know what's best. Have you got your teeth in?

KEMP. Yes.

MRS PLATT. Here. Have a sweet. Just a little one.

KEMP. Sister's looking.

We see SISTER MARQUAND *turn and walk out of the ward.*

MRS PLATT. There, she's gone. She won't be back. Gone to have her tea, I expect.

We follow SISTER MARQUAND *into the nurses' room, where she finds* SIMS *and* O'HARA *smoking.*

SISTER. Did anyone hear the racing results?

O'HARA. No, sister.

SISTER. Did you, Sims?

SIMS. Did I what?

SISTER. Back a horse? (SIMS *nods.*) What was it?

SIMS. Rambling Rose.

SISTER. Not a chance.

O'HARA. It's a good horse.

SISTER. It was – ten years ago!

O'HARA. I had a tip.

SISTER. Who did you get it from?

O'HARA. Staff-nurse O'Callaghan.

SISTER. Her tips will ruin you. She'll have you in the work-house. (*To* SIMS.) They go around in Dublin, giving each other these tips. Dead certs! They're gambling mad.

SIMS *titters dutifully*.

Throwing your money away, you are.

O'HARA. I often win.

SISTER. Bookies win oftener.

O'HARA. This tip was sound.

SIMS. I rather fancied it.

SISTER. Why?

SIMS. I've a sister called Rose. She lives in Birmingham.

SISTER. What a hole. (*To* O'HARA.) How much have you lost on the horses since Christmas?

O'HARA. Not much.

SISTER. How much?

O'HARA. I don't keep a book.

SISTER. All right, keep your hair on, O'Hara.

O'HARA. The friend that I had it from is reliable.

SISTER (*sniffs*). Working for the benefit of her health here, she is.

O'HARA (*sulkily*). I don't begrudge a few bob.

SISTER. As soon as you earn it, you throw it away. You're as bad, Sims. It gets me down. I'm soft hearted. I can't bear to see you throwing your hard-earned wages away.

SIMS. How much did you have on, sister?

SISTER. That's none of your business! You'd better get into the ward, O'Hara. There's no one about.

O'HARA (*stubbing out her cigarette*). Very good, sister.

Fade in to MR KEMP. *Sound of nurses talking, a loud laugh, a door slams.*

KEMP. It's noisy in here.

MRS PLATT. Of course it's noisy. You want to wear ear-plugs.

KEMP. Ear-plugs?

MRS PLATT. Yes, ear-plugs; I've had to wear them for years. Have a grape? Grapie? A little one?

KEMP. I had to have an injection last night, to make me sleep.

MRS PLATT. So you had to have an injection?

KEMP. Yes.

MRS PLATT. And you felt better after it, didn't you?

KEMP. I felt the same.

MRS PLATT. You're getting better!

KEMP. They had to give me oxygen.

MRS PLATT. Oxygen?

KEMP. Yes, I could scarcely breathe.

MRS PLATT. That would be nasty, I expect.

KEMP. Yes.

MRS PLATT. Still, you're feeling better?

KEMP. About the same.

MRS PLATT. We'll have you up and about in no time! (*Giving him sweet.*) This is a black one. You like them.

KEMP. It gets worse every night.

MRS PLATT. It's the dark. It always gets worse at night.

KEMP. They had a screen around me.

MRS PLATT. Fancy!

KEMP. They had the green light on!

MRS PLATT. Green?

KEMP. Green for go. Yes, they know when you're going to die.

MRS PLATT. You've got years ahead of you.

KEMP. They'll have to carry me out!

MRS PLATT. You mustn't say that.

KEMP. I shall be here until they carry me out.

MRS PLATT. We'll have you skipping about in no time!

KEMP. I won't bother you much longer.

MRS PLATT. I won't have that kind of talk, do you hear? You've got years ahead of you. What do you want to die for?

KEMP. I don't want to.

MRS PLATT. Well?

KEMP. But I'm going to.

MRS PLATT. You'll outlive us all! People live to a hundred every day. You'll feel better once the fine weather comes.

KEMP. I shan't see spring.

MRS PLATT. Oh yes, you will. You were always fond of spring flowers. I'll bring you a bunch in – when they get a bit cheaper. What do you say?

KEMP. I shan't see them.

MRS PLATT. Oh yes, you will!

KEMP. I've lost the use of it.

MRS PLATT. You've got to stop dwelling on *that* subject.

Have a grape?

KEMP. I don't want one.

MRS PLATT. Outside on the verandah's where you ought to
be. Outside in the fresh air.

KEMP. I do feel a bit low today.

MRS PLATT. I expect that Sister's been getting on your
nerves. No sense in getting on the patients' nerves – I shall
have a talk with her.

Sound of pneumatic drill from outside.

KEMP (*shouting*). It's noisy in here.

MRS PLATT. It is a bit. There! You've attracted nurse's
attention. She's coming over.

O'HARA. Everything all right?

MRS PLATT. I think he's a bit depressed today, nurse.

O'HARA. He mustn't be.

MRS PLATT. No.

O'HARA. What is there for him to be depressed about?

MRS PLATT. He's thinking of Mum – we lost her about this
time of the year.

O'HARA. I see. Is he comfortable?

MRS PLATT. I think so. Comfortable, are you? Nurse says are
you comfortable? (*He nods.*) With the nice weather coming
on, I was surprised he wasn't out on the verandah. That'd
be nice for him.

O'HARA. The verandah's draughty.

MRS PLATT. Is it?

O'HARA. Too draughty.

MRS PLATT. I expect you know best. I mean, it stands to
reason.

O'HARA. It faces north.

MRS PLATT. Does it?

O'HARA. It does.

MRS PLATT. That's a funny direction for a verandah to face.

O'HARA. It was the only place they could build it.

MRS PLATT. It must hardly get any sun?

O'HARA. It doesn't.

MRS PLATT. I wouldn't think that it did.

O'HARA. Three weeks we had the builders in and out.

MRS PLATT. It's not old, then?

O'HARA. It's very recent.

MRS PLATT. I thought I didn't remember it.

O'HARA. If it had been part of the original plan, they would never have built it facing north.

MRS PLATT. I suppose not. (*To* KEMP.) It's for your own good, you see, they've not put you on the verandah. Nurse says it faces north. He'll be easier in his mind now he knows.

Pause.

He was in Mary Ward at first, you know.

O'HARA. No, I didn't.

MRS PLATT (*sotto voce*). We thought we were going to lose him in Mary Ward. (*Loudly.*) Didn't we think we were going to lose you in Mary Ward?

KEMP. I wish I'd gone.

MRS PLATT. He worries me sometimes.

O'HARA. There's nothing to worry about.

MRS PLATT. And you'd let me know if there was?

O'HARA. Of course. (*To* KEMP.) As long as you keep cheerful, you'll be as right as rain.

MRS PLATT. Just remember that!

O'HARA. Of course he's not young . . .

MRS PLATT. Well, we'll just have to keep our fingers crossed. I'll see you again before I go, shall I?

O'HARA (*backing away*.) I expect so.

MRS PLATT. Good.

O'HARA. If there's anything else you want, just shout out.

MRS PLATT. You heard what she said? As long as you're cheerful, you'll be out in a month.

KEMP. Nothing much to be cheerful about. I'm losing weight – I'm as thin as a lath.

We follow O'HARA *to the nurses' room.* SIMS *is knitting.*

O'HARA. Is there a cup for me?

SIMS. Help yourself.

O'HARA. I'll put a bar of the fire on. I'm frozen. (*Switches on the second bar with her foot.*)

SIMS. How's number three? Still using the catheter?

O'HARA. Yes, he's depressed. (*Pouring tea out.*) He knows.

SIMS. Who told him?

O'HARA. He hasn't heard it from anyone. He just knows.

BROWN *enters, a well-built north country girl. She goes to the cupboard, takes a clean bottle out of it, covers it with a napkin and exits.*

Do you want a cup of tea? What's the matter with her?

SIMS. Sister Marquand's upset her.

O'HARA. Oh, Sister Marquand's got a lot to put up with.

SIMS. Still, you won't deny she's a first-class bitch. 'You're incompetent,' she said – out loud, just like that. 'You're incompetent!'

O'HARA. Mind you, that Brown deserves it. (*Reading Daily*

Sketch.) I see she was on T.V. last night.

SIMS. Who – Sister Marquand?

O'HARA. No.

SIMS. Oh, *her*. Yes, she was gorgeous.

O'HARA. I'm sorry I missed it.

SIMS. There'll be a repeat. You ought to have seen her – she knows how to handle horses.

O'HARA. On a horse was she? What kind?

SIMS. A big black one. She seems very fond of big, black horses.

O'HARA. Black, you say?

SIMS. Yes.

O'HARA. Here it says grey.

SIMS. Never!

O'HARA. Here it is.

SIMS. Well, it came out black on the screen.

BROWN *re-enters*.

BROWN. Where's tea? (*She sits down*.)

SIMS. Are you upset?

BROWN. Upset?

SIMS. You seem upset.

BROWN. There'll be somebody upset before long. If she says one more word to me . . .

O'HARA. What's the matter?

BROWN. That Sister Bloody Marquand's too fond of finding fault. That's what's the matter.

O'HARA. Go on. She's all right.

SIMS. Got it in for you, hasn't she?

BROWN (*stirring her tea*). I'd like to show that woman up!
It's time somebody told her where she got off.

O'HARA. You and who else?

BROWN. I'm not staying here all my life, and before I leave, I
shall make her jump! Just let her open her mouth once,
that's all. I'll have that hat half way down her throat!

O'HARA. You'll what?

SIMS. She's a difficult woman.

BROWN. Difficult! Just let me get a win on the pools, that's
all I ask, and I'll have her running through that ward as if a
regiment of Gurkhas was after her!

O'HARA. Tell her, not us.

BROWN. I will.

O'HARA. You wouldn't say that to her face.

BROWN. Wouldn't I?

O'HARA. That Sister would eat you.

BROWN. She'd what?

O'HARA. She'd make mincemeat of you. She'll eat you with
salad.

BROWN. What! I'll give Matron notice in writing. 'Matron,'
I'll say, 'I hereby give notice that on such-and-such a day
I intend to do Sister Marquand.'

SIMS. And what will she say?

BROWN. She'll say: 'Go ahead, Nurse Brown. She deserves a
good belting. She's had it coming for years.' (*Pause.*) I'll
have her guts for garters.

O'HARA. Don't make me laugh!

BROWN. I wasn't in the Girl Guides for nothing.

The telephone buzzes.

O'HARA. That'll be for me. (*Answers it.*) Yes? Yes. (*Replaces
receiver.*) Tea.

SIMS. You on duty?

O'HARA. I'm serving tea and I'm going. I shan't be sorry.

BROWN. If you see your friend on the way out, give her my love.

O'HARA. Are you serious?

BROWN. What do you think?

Exit O'HARA.

SIMS. You were a fool to say that.

BROWN. What?

SIMS. In front of O'Hara.

BROWN. What can I do – I'm so impetuous.

SIMS. It'll go back. She'll go and tell Marquand every word you've been saying. See if I'm not right.

BROWN. I'm crying!

SIMS. That's what she'll do.

BROWN. She's welcome.

Enter FAZAKERLEY, *a tall coloured girl.*

FAZAKERLEY. It's hot in here. Mind if I put this off? (*Kicks off fire with her heel.*)

BROWN. Let her tell Marquand, I'm independent. I'm not crawling – my old job's waiting for me. I can always go back to making brown paper bags!

FAZAKERLEY. You couldn't get a job making beds!

BROWN. Still with us, I see. Aren't you, dear? She's a nice girl, though.

SIMS. O'Hara is a terrible bitch.

BROWN. You're telling me nothing I didn't know.

SIMS. Those convent-trained girls are murder.

BROWN. It's the upbringing. Nuns are a dozy lot. No wonder

they turn out cretins like that O'Hara.

Dissolve to O'HARA *pushing tea-trolley into the ward.*
Over her shoulder we see MRS PLATT *talking to* KEMP.

MRS PLATT. Janice sends her love. And was there anything
special you wanted?

KEMP. No.

MRS PLATT. She's doing well, Janice is.

KEMP. I hope she's behaving herself.

MRS PLATT. Mrs Flackwell wishes to be remembered.

KEMP. Who?

MRS PLATT. Mrs Flackwell. Her with the bad leg.

KEMP. Ah.

MRS PLATT. She says they're all asking after you down at the
club. You're remembered, you see. She asked about visiting
time.

KEMP. Did she.

MRS PLATT. So she'll be coming along, I expect. They all
think a lot of you. Don't pretend different. She hasn't forgot
all you did for her when their Stanley died. No. She hasn't.

KEMP. All that fog down by the cemetery.

MRS PLATT. I don't think she's been the same since. It was
a shock to her system. Some people would be in a mental
home with what Mrs Flackwell's had to put up with. It
would of given some people a break-down. Not her, she's
one of the best. (*Pause.*) I'll tell her you're better. (*Pause.*)
You wouldn't want not to be remembered to her, would
you?

KEMP. No. She's been a good friend to me.

MRS PLATT. She has.

KEMP. Say goodbye to her for me.

MRS PLATT. You are in a mood today, aren't you?

KEMP. I'm sinking.

MRS PLATT. You'll see Mrs Flackwell again.

KEMP. No, I shan't be here much longer.

MRS PLATT. You'll see all of us underground.

KEMP. No.

MRS PLATT. Yes, you will. Don't upset yourself. Here comes
nurse with your tea. Sit up then! Sit up. There you are.
Mind your hands! It's on wheels – have you noticed? I
expect you have. It's on wheels to make it easier – you
wheel it backwards or forwards, as you like. (*Pause.*)
I could do with a cup myself.

KEMP. Ask her.

MRS PLATT. No.

KEMP. Go on, she won't mind.

MRS PLATT. Tea is for patients. I'm only a visitor. What
would she think?

O'HARA *arrives with the trolley.*

Hallo, nurse. He's ready now for his tea.

O'HARA. All right, is he?

MRS PLATT. Having a bit of a moan. That's his way. It's the
time of the year.

O'HARA. Cake or bread and butter?

KEMP. I don't mind.

MRS PLATT. Make up your mind; nurse is waiting.

KEMP. It's all the same to me.

MRS PLATT. You see how he is? (*To* KEMP.) There are other
patients waiting.

O'HARA. No. He's the last. Cake or bread and butter?

MRS PLATT. Come on, have a nice piece of bread and butter?
A nice piece of cake then? A piece of brown bread? Don't

you fancy it?

KEMP. No.

MRS PLATT. Just a cup of tea, nurse.

O'HARA. Here you are.

MRS PLATT. He's always ready for that. I've never known
him say no to a cup of tea. That's right – hold it steady.
Don't spill any, or nurse will tell you off. Won't you, nurse?
She'll tell you off. (*Silence.*) Can you hear music?

O'HARA. It's from the street. Is it annoying you?

Sound of accordion playing 'Pale Hands I Loved'.

MRS PLATT. I don't mind.

O'HARA. I'll close the window.

MRS PLATT. Not if you're supposed to keep it open. He plays
well, that accordionist.

O'HARA. Sure you won't have something to eat?

KEMP. No.

O'HARA. It's a long time to supper.

MRS PLATT. Have a nice cake?

O'HARA. Will you?

MRS PLATT. Have this bun – look, it has icing on. You'd like
that, wouldn't you?

KEMP. If you want.

MRS PLATT. It's not what I want at all. It's what you want.
(*To nurse.*) Is he like this all the time? (*To* KEMP.) You
make your own choice.

KEMP. I'll have that one.

O'HARA. The plain one? That'll be nice.

MRS PLATT. It's not very tasty. (*Pause.*) I couldn't find him at
first.

O'HARA. Why not?

MRS PLATT. They'd moved him. I thought at first that they'd moved him back into Mary Ward.

O'HARA. Is that where he was?

MRS PLATT. He was. But I don't think it suited him. I should say, nurse, it's given him a new lease of life being in this ward. There isn't a doubt of it. He's looking more of his old self. He has a definite flush in his cheeks.

Close-up of KEMP *eating cake.*

MRS PLATT (*rummaging in a bag*). I brought these eggs for him. Shall I give them to Sister, or will you take charge of them?

O'HARA. I'll take them if you like.

MRS PLATT. I've marked them.

O'HARA. That's right.

MRS PLATT. I hope I've done the right thing, but I wouldn't want someone else getting his eggs. You wouldn't do it on purpose, I know, but accidents happen. I wouldn't begrudge another patient an egg; it's just that I brought them for him, and I'd like to think of him getting them.

She produces a book.

I brought him this book. (*Pause.*) I don't suppose that he'll read it.

O'HARA. Put it there on his locker.

MRS PLATT. I'm not sure whether this one is light enough. It has to be something light or he won't be bothered. Some of these books nowadays make me frightened. (*Pause.*) You wouldn't think that a book could have that effect, would you? But it does. I usually ask a friend of mine if she's read it, and if she has then it's all right. You'd wonder why they print some of those books. I picked one up last week, *Life in the Space Age*. I ask you! Who wants to read about life in the Space Age? Still, I suppose it's all for the best. We've got to move with the times, haven't we? Move or be left behind.

O'HARA. Have you finished with your cup?

KEMP. Ah.

MRS PLATT. Did you enjoy it?

KEMP. Yes.

MRS PLATT. Well, that's something to be thankful for.

O'HARA. Give me your cup.

MRS PLATT. The nurse wants your cup!

KEMP. I'm tired.

O'HARA. That's a good sign!

KEMP. I'm dying!

MRS PLATT. Have you finished?

KEMP. Yes.

MRS PLATT. Then give nurse your plate. Do you want
    something else?

KEMP. No.

O'HARA. That's right.

MRS PLATT. Sure?

KEMP. Yes.

MRS PLATT. That'll be all then. He enjoyed his tea. You
    didn't want to have any, did you? If we hadn't nearly forced
    you, you'd never have had any. Isn't that so? And I'm sure
    you're feeling the better for it. Hurry up with that cup now;
    nurse wants to clear away. (*Pause.*) I shall be having my tea
    when I get in.

KEMP. Nurse . . .

O'HARA. What is it?

MRS PLATT. He wants you!

KEMP. How old are you?

O'HARA. Twenty-two.

KEMP. If I live to July, I'll be eighty-five.

MRS PLATT. Of course you'll live to July. You'll live for years!

O'HARA. Well, what do you make of that? Now, you're not to upset yourself.

MRS PLATT. I'm glad you're here, nurse, to reassure him. He won't take a scrap of notice of me.

KEMP. You can't imagine what it's like to be old, nurse. Look at that hand. (*Close-up of hand.*) It's not a hand at all.

O'HARA. It's not?

KEMP. It's more like a claw!

MRS PLATT. He will keep saying things like that.

KEMP. Everything passes. I shan't see another summer.

MRS PLATT. Of course you will. Won't he, nurse?

O'HARA. He will.

KEMP. I'm dying –

O'HARA. Here, let me make you comfortable. (*She plumps his pillow.*) That's better. It makes all the difference. (*Pause.*) What's this? Who's been giving him toffee?

MRS PLATT. Toffee?

O'HARA (*holding it up*). There's a whole tinful here.

MRS PLATT. He likes something sweet.

O'HARA. But he isn't supposed to have it. I'm surprised at you. I thought you had more sense. I don't know what Sister would say. She'd give you the rough edge of her tongue.

MRS PLATT. It won't happen again.

O'HARA. Promise me?

MRS PLATT. I will.

O'HARA. Some of you visitors – I think you want to kill the patients.

MRS PLATT. One toffee can't do much harm.

O'HARA. You might as well give him poison. If you don't believe me, ask Sister!

The old man belches.

MRS PLATT (*after looking at him*). He never seemed to get on well with the nurses in Mary Ward. I expect he got on their nerves.

O'HARA (*sotto voce*). He gets on mine sometimes.

MRS PLATT. I know. It's no fun being a nurse, is it?

O'HARA. It's not bad. I must be off with these dishes or Sister will be chasing me up.

MRS PLATT. No fun. These young girls think it's fun. They read these books about nurses getting off with the doctors, and they think it's true. They think nurses have nothing better to do than to fill their heads with thoughts about men. Man-mad they are! You nurses have got other things to think about.

Dissolve to close-up of Swann's Way being read by FAZAKERLEY.

BROWN. I prefer her sister.

SIMS. She isn't bad. I'd like to shake hands with one of them.

BROWN. How are you getting on?

SIMS (*holding up her knitting*). I'm at the half-way mark. Her hubby is some kind of relation of *her* hubby, isn't he?

BROWN. Yes. I'm against it myself.

SIMS. Still, they seem to be managing.

BROWN. What's that you're knitting?

SIMS. A cardigan.

BROWN. Never! It's the wrong shape.

SIMS. I followed the pattern.

BROWN. Who are you knitting it for – an octopus?

SIMS. I've checked it against the pattern in *Woman's Friend.*

BROWN. You can't always trust them. You've got the wrong needles in for a kick-off.

SIMS. You're trying to discourage me.

BROWN. I'm trying to help.

SIMS. I'm using the same needles my mum used.

BROWN. What's the wool?

SIMS. Three-ply. Number nine needles.

BROWN. They're never nine. They're twelve!

SIMS. My mum bought them by mistake.

BROWN. She's as bad as you are. Oh, well, you know what you're doing. It's your look-out. You'll have a cardigan like a herring net. Still, you can always use it as a mop.

O'HARA *enters pushing the trolley with used tea-things. Also a bowl with the visitor's eggs.*

O'HARA. Where's Cameron?

BROWN. She'll be in.

O'HARA. What's the time?

SIMS. Twenty-five past. She'll be here in a minute.

O'HARA *pushes trolley off into the kitchen.*

That O'Hara's a proper bitch.

BROWN. You surprise me.

SIMS. You won't let this go any further?

BROWN. Trust me, Mary.

SIMS. Fazakerley?

BROWN. Don't bother about her. She's glued to the pages.

FAZAKERLEY (*looking up from her book*). Do you mind?

BROWN. She's had her nose in between those two covers so long it's beginning to look like a book-mark. What is it?

(*Twisting her head round to see the title.*) *Swann's Way.*
I didn't know you were interested in birds?

FAZAKERLEY. I'm not.

BROWN. What's it about then?

FAZAKERLEY. You wouldn't be interested.

BROWN. She thinks I'm dead ignorant. Take a look at her
eyes. Aren't they blood-shot? It's all this reading. You'll kill
yourself, dear. Honest. And she looked so fresh at first. We
all noticed it when she came. But what were you saying?

Pause.

SIMS. You remember when Cameron left that dish-cloth
wrapped around the hot-water bottle in the bed of the
appendix patient?

BROWN. Do I? Marquand nearly wet herself, didn't she? Eh?
Tried to blame it on me. She rushed in here effing and
blinding. 'I'll have you up before Matron,' she said. Oh,
she's wicked when she starts.

SIMS. Well, it was O'Hara put the poison down. Told Sister
Marquand Cameron was responsible.

BROWN. You can't trust Paddies. They're a two-faced lot.

O'HARA *re-enters.*

O'HARA. Half a dozen eggs for number three. I've left them
on the draining board.

SIMS. Who brought them?

O'HARA. His daughter.

BROWN. Every time she comes she brings eggs; I think she
must lay them herself.

O'HARA (*sitting down*). I'm done. I'm finished. I shan't be
sorry to put my feet up. You know, it's a funny thing, I feel
ready to drop today.

CAMERON *enters. She is a thin, pale Scots girl. She walks
to the table, sits heavily in a chair, buries her head in her*

hands, and bursts into tears.

BROWN. Hey, up!

SIMS. What is it?

O'HARA. What's the matter?

CAMERON (*through her tears*). Leave me alone.

SIMS. Who's been upsetting you?

BROWN. Is it Marquand?

CAMERON. No.

BROWN. I bet it is.

CAMERON. It isn't.

O'HARA. What's wrong then?

CAMERON (*sits and searches for a handkerchief, and dries her eyes*). I'm up the spout.

BROWN. Is that all?

Fade out.

ACT TWO

The following morning. MR KEMP *has been moved into a bed out on the verandah, a greenhouse-like construction. There are cane chairs, folded screen in one corner.* MR BASSET, *a patient in a dressing gown, is sitting in one of the chairs listening to a pair of earphones.*

KEMP. They said you were dead.

BASSET. Eh?

KEMP. They said you were dead.

BASSET. Yes, she's made my bed. She made it this morning. Well, she's made it several times since.

KEMP. No, DEAD! They said you'd passed out.

BASSET. She comes up to me and says, 'Here, let's make you comfortable.' She's done it several times – maybe six.

KEMP. She's taken a fancy to you.

BASSET. Eh? (*Removes his earphones.*)

KEMP. She's taken a fancy to you. You'd better watch out.

BASSET. Yes.

KEMP. You want to watch out. (*Pause.*) They said you were dead. I saw them flying about. I asked one of them what was the matter.

BASSET. Yes.

KEMP. I was surprised. Very surprised.

BASSET. Why?

KEMP. I don't know. I was, that's all. You didn't look as though you were going to pass out.

BASSET. No.

KEMP. You looked a bit under the weather, but not on your last legs. No.

BASSET. I felt a bit under the weather.

KEMP. You looked it. Yes. (*Pause.*) It would have been a shock if you'd gone. I mean, you don't expect that sort of thing to happen – not in front of your face. I must say, they all took it very well considering. I admired that nurse – the way she kept her head. (*Taking out his pipe and filling it.*)

BASSET. They've had second thoughts then about your pipe?

KEMP. Yes. I think they want to kill me.

BASSET. First they tell you one thing and then another. How's that? Eh? How's that? You don't know whether you're on your head or your heels with them half the time.

KEMP. They want to do me in.

BASSET. No, it's because you're better.

KEMP (*darkly*). Is it?

BASSET. I expect so.

KEMP. I've got no confidence in them. None at all. I wonder sometimes if we're safe in the hands of these nurses. Look at old Wilkins – talking about getting up on Friday. (*Pause.*) Saturday he was dead.

BASSET. That was heart.

KEMP. So *they* say.

BASSET. He'd always had trouble with it.

KEMP. He'd had a few words with the Sister on Friday. On Saturday he was dead. You can't put it plainer than that.

BASSET (*putting on his earphones again*). You want to be careful. She'll sue you for libel.

KEMP. Anything on?

BASSET. No. (*Pause.*) There was a nice play on yesterday.

KEMP. I like a nice play. I must have missed it.

BASSET. You were asleep.

KEMP. You ought to have wakened me. You've let me miss some nice things. Many a time I wake up and you tell me about something good that's been on. (*Pause.*) I'm sorry I missed it.

BASSET. Yes, it was better than that Third Programme she's always got on.

KEMP. Ah, she's one of the highbrows. Likes classical music.

BASSET. She's fond of the classics.

KEMP. Ah well, it's the way these people manage their lives. Live and let live, I say. (*Pause.*) What are you listening to?

BASSET. Music.

KEMP. What kind of music?

BASSET. Classical.

KEMP. You ought to ask her to switch over.

BASSET. She wouldn't like that.

Pause.

KEMP. Good play on yesterday, was there, then?

BASSET. Very.

KEMP. What time would that be?

BASSET. When you were asleep. About five.

KEMP. My daughter was thinking about taking up Opera one time. All for it she was.

BASSET. That the one who comes in to see you? (KEMP *nods*.) Is she your eldest?

KEMP. Eldest living.

BASSET. The eldest living?

KEMP. Yes.

BASSET. How many more did you have?

KEMP. Nine.

BASSET. A big family.

Pause.

KEMP. Not all of them lived.

BASSET. It was the conditions.

KEMP. Yes. Conditions have changed.

BASSET. You had a struggle to bring them up then.

KEMP. It's all changed now. It's different. I think the first we had was a boy. He died of what they call meningitis. Then we had twins. I believe they came next. Anne and Winifred. They lived until they were twelve. Then we lost them within a week of each other. I can't remember the cause. (*Pause.*) I knew at the time, of course. I asked the doctor straight out what had happened. He told me.

BASSET. What was it?

KEMP. I can't recall what he said now. It's a long time ago. Before you were born.

BASSET. Must have been. What happened about your daughter?

KEMP. Ah yes. We did think of having her trained.

BASSET. She'd set her heart on the singing then?

KEMP. Yes. We took her along to that Madame Valerini. You've heard of her?

BASSET. No.

KEMP. She was very well-known at the time. She had a voice that could break wine-glasses. That's what they said. I often wondered if it was true. I would have asked her, but I didn't like to. Not that she would have minded. She wasn't that type. But it seemed too personal, so I didn't.

BASSET. You hear so many stories. You can't believe half of them.

KEMP. I remember we took a cab from the corner to
Madame's studio. Just before the Great War, it was. Only
cost us a shilling. Not much, is it?

BASSET. No.

KEMP. It's not much. Well, it wasn't far. We could have
walked, but we thought Madame might not like us to. It
wasn't done in those days. In those days it wasn't done to
arrive at anyone's door on foot. It was more than your life
was worth. It's gone out now. Nobody bothers.

BASSET. It must have been a hard custom.

KEMP. It was. It laid a heavy burden on the Working Classes.
I always maintain it was done on purpose. You'll never
persuade me different. It was deliberate policy.

BASSET. I can believe it.

KEMP. You came too late. You've no conception. The ruling
classes of those days, they made some impossible rules.
Impossible. They couldn't keep up with half of them
themselves. And they used to drink a lot. Drink rots the
brain, you know.

BASSET. No, I didn't.

KEMP. You could tell when you saw them.

BASSET. It's different now.

KEMP. Very different.

BASSET. What happened to this daughter of yours?

KEMP. Madame put us into a waiting-room when we arrived.
She seemed a bit cross about something. I expect one of her
students had upset her. Very irritating they can be, these
students. 'What can I do for you?' she said. So I told her. I
told her Daisy had set her heart on singing. She listened to
every word I said – she was a good listener.

BASSET. She'd need to be.

KEMP. What's that?

BASSET. Nothing.

Pause.

KEMP. She took Daisy into the next room. We could hear
them. No getting away from it, Daisy had done better. That
day she didn't have a fair chance. All the same Madame
seemed very pleased with her. 'You have a very nice voice,'
she said. Just like that.

BASSET. What happened then?

KEMP. Nothing. It was just before the Great War, you see, and
Madame had a lot on her plate. With her concerts, her
students, her private tuition, she hadn't the time. So we had
to let it go. We let it go at that. Daisy seemed to lose
interest. I'd warned her, 'You've got the rest of your life in
front of you.' She didn't see it that way, though. She moped.

Pause.

There's nothing usual on at five.

BASSET. There was yesterday.

KEMP. Nothing usual. Only for kids.

BASSET. There were three little girls in this play.

KEMP. Nice. Very nice.

BASSET. No, as I remember one of them was a boy.

KEMP. Weren't you sure?

BASSET (*ignoring this*). They had white dresses on.

KEMP. White dresses?

BASSET. Yes.

KEMP. I like a little girl in a white dress. Were they going to a
party?

BASSET. I don't know.

KEMP. Was it Christmas?

BASSET. No.

KEMP. Somebody's birthday? What were they celebrating?

BASSET. It didn't say.

Pause.

KEMP. What was it about?

BASSET. It was about this Major –

KEMP. In the army, was he? I wish I'd heard it.

BASSET. He'd been in the army some time previous.

KEMP. You gathered that?

BASSET. Yes. He took them back to his house and locked them up in a cupboard.

KEMP. This Major?

BASSET. Yes.

KEMP. He must have been unbalanced. (*Pause.*) Did they give a reason?

BASSET. No, it was on the spur of the moment.

KEMP. No sane man would do a thing like that. How did they get out?

BASSET. They got out through a door in the back.

KEMP. Of the cupboard?

BASSET. Yes.

KEMP. Oh. Did it hold your interest?

BASSET. Yes.

KEMP. I wish I'd heard it. I'm sorry I missed it. Sounds interesting.

Enter SISTER MARQUAND.

SISTER. Have you got enough clothes on?

KEMP. Yes.

SISTER. Have you changed your pyjamas, Mr Basset?

BASSET. No.

SISTER. Why not? Why haven't you changed your pyjamas?

BASSET. It never occurred to me.

SISTER. Didn't you have a bath last night?

BASSET. No.

SISTER. Why not?

BASSET. Nobody said anything.

SISTER. Were you excused?

BASSET. I don't know. I don't expect so.

SISTER. Did you change them last week?

BASSET. I forget.

SISTER. What do you mean? Did you have a bath last week?

BASSET. I can't remember.

Long pause.

SISTER. I see. You must have a very short memory. Now, Mr
Basset, this is no way to carry on.

BASSET. No.

SISTER. I'd like to know what you're playing at, Mr Basset.
It's not a joke. You've not had a bath for a fortnight. You
haven't changed your pyjamas. Did you have a bath when
you were admitted?

BASSET. Yes, I had two.

SISTER. You had two baths on the same day?

BASSET. Yes.

SISTER. And you think that keeps you clean for a fortnight?

BASSET. No.

SISTER. I should like to know just what you do think, Mr
Basset. (*Nods.*) Very well. (*Turns to* KEMP.) Is your bed
quite comfortable?

KEMP. Yes, thank you.

SISTER. Are you sure? It doesn't look comfortable. (*Goes to door and calls:*) Sims! Sims! Come here. (*Coming back to the bed.*) Did you see the doctor this morning?

KEMP. Yes.

SISTER (*nodding her head*). Have you had a movement?

KEMP. Not yet.

SISTER. Hadn't you better?

KEMP. I don't usually so early. I thought I'd just wait and see.

Enter SIMS.

SISTER. This patient's bed isn't comfortable, nurse.

SIMS. No, sister.

SISTER. Make it.

SIMS (*helping him out of bed*). Here. Sit in this chair.

SISTER. Your daughter is coming to see you this morning. Have you got your pipe?

KEMP. Yes.

SISTER. Be careful you don't set yourself on fire. This patient hasn't had a movement this morning, nurse.

SIMS. No?

SISTER. In future I want you to tell nurse, Mr Kemp. And I want you, nurse, to let me know.

SIMS. Yes.

SISTER. Very good.

She goes off.

SIMS. There, that's better.

KEMP. It was quite comfy before.

SIMS. Sister knows best! (*Helping him back into bed.*) There! You'll find that better.

KEMP. Thank you.

She goes towards the door.

BASSET. Nurse!

SIMS. What?

BASSET. Can you switch the wireless over? It's on the Third.

SIMS. Is it? The Third isn't on in the morning.

BASSET. Oh. Then it can't be. I thought it was.

SIMS. Not in the morning.

Exit.

BASSET (*after a pause*). Have you tried those pills for your movements?

KEMP. When I was in Mary Ward, my daughter brought in something of the sort. The sister found them. Took them away, she did. 'Don't let me catch you with those,' she said. 'Never!' It seems they were bad for the inside.

BASSET. Ever tried Monastery Herbs?

KEMP. No.

BASSET. I'm a believer in herbs. Look at the Gypsies. When they feel in need, they just dig up a herb or two. I swear by herbs.

KEMP. What shaving soap do you use?

BASSET. Brushless.

KEMP. I use Coal Tar. I always have – I find it refreshing. I can't stick that brushless. I tried some once. It brought up a rash. I forget its name. Very bad I was. (*Pause.*) When I shaved first, they didn't use soap. I was still at school.

BASSET. Things were different in those days.

KEMP. Vastly. When I walked down the road, I could hardly lift my feet. Very heavy, the boots was in those days. (*Pause.*) Many children had nothing to put on their feet at all. I was seven when I went to school. Thrash, thrash, thrash! I can see the master now, pulling a lad across his desk. (*Pause.*) That memory has stayed with me vividly. (*Indicating earphones.*) What's on?

BASSET. Nothing.

KEMP. Nothing?

BASSET. It's dead.

Enter NURSE BROWN.

BROWN. Which of you is it for a bath? (*Silence.*) Come along. Which of you is it?

BASSET. You must know. You must have been told.

BROWN. No, I didn't wait to ask. Is it you, Mr Basset? Now then, what's your game? Sister came in here –

BASSET. I know she did.

BROWN. Did she tell you for a bath, Mr Basset, or didn't she? (*Pause.*) Did you have one last night?

BASSET. I don't think so.

BROWN. Then she means you.

She goes to door. MRS PLATT *stands outside.*

Oh, good morning, Mrs Platt. (*Turning.*) Be ready for you in a jiffy, Mr Basset.

Exit.

MRS PLATT (*coming forward*). They moved you then.

KEMP. Yes. This is Mr Basset.

MRS PLATT. How do you do? I'm not stopping long. How are you?

KEMP. All right.

MRS PLATT. Not cold out here, are you?

KEMP. No.

MRS PLATT. No, you're looking better. In yourself, I mean. Did they give you your egg?

KEMP. Yes.

MRS PLATT. Only one? (*He nods.*) You'd think they'd give you more than one, wouldn't you? It's not as though they had to pay for them. (*Pause.*) I spoke to that man who plays the accordion.

KEMP. Did you?

MRS PLATT. Yes. He plays so well that I felt I ought to. I felt it incumbent upon me. I told him what I thought of his playing. But I told him I didn't think he ought to play outside hospitals. I told him he ought to think of the patients. I'm surprised no one's complained before now. (*Pause.*) He's a war veteran.

KEMP. A war veteran, is he? Did you get his name?

MRS PLATT. Think he might have been a friend of yours?

KEMP. Might have been.

MRS PLATT. He didn't say his name. Couldn't be expected to.

KEMP. Although I never knew anybody who played the accordion.

MRS PLATT. Didn't you?

KEMP. I never did.

MRS PLATT. Him and me had quite a chat. He was telling me – out in all weathers. He stopped playing while he talked – well, it stands to reason. I think, if it's wet, he nips into the pub on the corner.

KEMP. I don't blame him.

MRS PLATT. Neither do I. He lost three of his fingers in Flanders. So he said. Well, I suppose he might have been spinning me a tale. But he never misses them, he says. In fact he thinks it improved his playing. He plays very loud. (*Pause.*) I told him about you being wounded. On the Somme, wasn't it?

KEMP. Didn't I tell you?

MRS PLATT. That's where I thought it was.

KEMP. It was not on the Somme.

MRS PLATT. Where was it then?

KEMP. Not on the Somme.

MRS PLATT. No? Where was it? I'd like to have a word with him on my way out – correct the impression.

Silence.

Well if you won't tell me, you won't. You don't deserve to have visitors. You don't. I'm sorry I came. Is he like this with you, Mr Basset? I wonder how you put up with him. Where was it? Where were you wounded?

Silence.

Well now, we know where we stand. I shan't forget this in a hurry. You don't know where it was. Like them all, you've forgotten. (*Pause.*) They forget, they do.

KEMP. I've not forgotten.

MRS PLATT. Oh. Then where was it?

KEMP. It was never the same again. No. Never. I might have been killed. And what was it all for? They're names now – all names: Eddie and Albert, and Ron and Dave. I was only wounded. But some of them died. Shall I tell you something?

BASSET. What?

KEMP. They gave me a medal. I lost it when we were bombed out last time. I ask you – what kind of people are they? They give you a medal in one war and blow it to bits in the next. I wrote them a letter. They never replied. I might as well never have bothered.

MRS PLATT (*transferring her attention to* BASSET). Is your name by any chance Reg, Mr Basset?

BASSET. Yes.

MRS PLATT. Is it? You wouldn't know me.

KEMP. What did I get wounded for? People die, don't they? They die. All this talking, but people die. (*Pause.*) My lungs have never been the same. I've had pain.

MRS PLATT. You don't know me, do you? But I've just realised, I know you. It came to me suddenly. Isn't your wife a tall lady with glasses, name of Irene, belongs to the Mere End social club?

BASSET. Yes.

KEMP. They forget. Talk, talk, talk. Men die, and they talk. They lay wreaths, they have services, they sell poppies. What a waste it's all been, what a waste.

MRS PLATT. She must have spoken to you about me. I've been to your house.

BASSET. Have you?

MRS PLATT. Yes. She's an active woman, isn't she? Keeps on her feet.

BASSET. She's a lovely woman.

KEMP. I don't think it's worth it. I don't think it's worth a single death.

MRS PLATT. You work for the Council, don't you?

BASSET. That's right.

MRS PLATT. How long is it? Forty-three years?

BASSET. Forty-five.

MRS PLATT. Irene's often told me. She's proud of your record. It isn't often you meet people nowadays who take a pride in their work. That's what makes them so discontented. And you take a pride in your work, don't you? I can see you do.

KEMP. That's why he's here.

MRS PLATT. On the dust-bins, weren't you?

BASSET (*indignantly*). A picker!

MRS PLATT. Oh, is that different?

BASSET. I should just think it is. (*Proudly*.) At the Ashburton Road Refuse Disposal Depot.

MRS PLATT. I believe your wife mentioned it to me.

BASSET. I've been working inside for the past few years.

MRS PLATT. It must have slipped my mind.

BASSET. Yes.

MRS PLATT. It must be nice for you inside – out of the wet?
Nice and dry?

BASSET. You're right there.

MRS PLATT. Yes, we can't do with too much outside weather
as we get older. The damp does nobody any good. What do
you pick?

BASSET. Rags, mostly.

MRS PLATT. Must be worth a fortune!

BASSET. Old furniture covers, scraps of dress material, worn-
out dish-cloths.

MRS PLATT. A gold-mine!

BASSET. They fetch up to thirteen quid a ton.

MRS PLATT. Fancy.

BASSET. Then there's the paper.

MRS PLATT. Paper as well?

BASSET. If it's clean.

MRS PLATT. Do they pay you when you're off work?

BASSET. Definitely.

MRS PLATT. I'm glad to hear that. Yes, I'm glad you've had
no trouble with them. (*Pause.*) The dust must be bad for
your chest.

BASSET. They make every effort to eliminate it.

MRS PLATT. What are the men like? They look a bit rough,
some of them. I hope you don't mind my saying that?

BASSET. No, I don't mind. (*Pause.*) Funny chaps, some of
them.

MRS PLATT. Are they quarrelsome?

BASSET. Yes.

MRS PLATT. I thought so. They look that way.

BASSET. It's their work makes them.

MRS PLATT. It's an essential service. No doubt about that. Do you get a bath where you work?

BASSET. What?

MRS PLATT. Do you get a bath?

BASSET (*dangerously*). You're the second person who's asked me that question today.

MRS PLATT. I was just interested.

BASSET. Baths. That's all they can think about.

MRS PLATT. I just enquired. (*Pause.*) I expect you'd need one.

BASSET. Who says I would?

MRS PLATT. It stands to reason.

BASSET. We keep clean.

MRS PLATT. It must be difficult.

BASSET. We're as clean as the next man!

MRS PLATT (*anxiously*). I'm sure you are.

BASSET. Baths, baths, baths all the time. Anybody'd think you pong. (*Pause.*) I don't pong. Do I?

MRS PLATT. I've noticed nothing.

BASSET. The general public know practically nothing.

Enter BROWN.

BROWN. Your bath's ready now. Where are your clean pyjamas? (*Pause.*) Did you say you had clean pyjamas? Do you want them aired?

BASSET. No.

BROWN. They are clean?

BASSET. Clean? Yes, of course they're clean.

BROWN. And they've been aired?

BASSET. They're new.

BROWN. You haven't worn them before?

BASSET. No.

BROWN. Come along then.

BASSET. Do I smell?

BROWN. I wouldn't know.

BASSET. Just because you're a picker, they think that you smell. A picker isn't an ordinary dustman. I don't smell.

BROWN. Look here – what have you got against taking a bath.

BASSET. I don't smell.

BROWN. Come along now – get busy with that soap.

Enter SISTER.

SISTER. What's the matter, nurse?

BROWN. Patient refuses to have a bath.

BASSET. I don't need one.

SISTER. You must have a bath.

BASSET. You can't force me.

SISTER. You've no choice. It's regulations. Where are your clean pyjamas? Are they in your locker?

BASSET. Yes.

SISTER. And are they aired? Have you asked nurse to air them for you?

BASSET. No.

SISTER. What prevented you?

BASSET. I didn't think.

SISTER. Are they in your locker?

BASSET. Yes.

SISTER. Top or bottom?

BASSET. I don't know.

SISTER. Are they thick?

BASSET. I haven't examined them.

SISTER. They may be thin?

BASSET. They may be.

SISTER. They may be unsuitable? Does your wife know this?
  (*He nods.*) When is she visiting you?

BASSET. Tomorrow.

SISTER. Is she on the telephone? Can she be reached?

BASSET. No.

SISTER. She can't?

BASSET. She can't be contacted.

SISTER (*with a sigh*). I don't think you're trying, Mr Basset.
  How can you hope to get well, if you go on like this? We're
  here to help you. You understand?

  Silence.

  Did you see the doctor this morning, Mr Kemp?

KEMP. Yes.

SISTER. After breakfast?

KEMP. After breakfast.

SISTER. In here?

KEMP. In the ward.

SISTER I see. Come along now, Mr Basset, that bath is getting
  cold. What have you got against it?

BASSET. I'm not against it.

SISTER. You seem to be. Are you sure that you're feeling well? Have you taken Mr Basset's temperature this morning, nurse?

BROWN. No, sister.

SISTER. Take it now. (*Pause.*) Now, Mr Basset, why do you refuse to take a bath?

BASSET (*with the thermometer in his mouth*). Me arteries won't let the blood through.

SISTER. That's quite beside the point.

BASSET. Besides that, I don't smell. Do I?

SISTER. Does he?

BROWN. No.

SISTER. But you need a bath. (*As though the matter is quite disposed of.*) Leave your dirty pyjamas in the bathroom. Did you take your sedative this morning?

BASSET. No.

SISTER. Why not?

BASSET. I threw it away.

SISTER (*after a silence*). Now, why did you do that, Mr Basset? Why do you think the doctor prescribed these things? They're to help you.

BASSET. I can't think clearly.

BROWN. Where did you throw it?

BASSET. Out of the window.

SISTER. This is inexcusable behaviour, Mr Basset. You know that, don't you? I shall have to speak to the doctor about it. Now come along now – no more nonsense. Nurse, take his arm.

They lead him out in silence.

KEMP. He does smell, you know.

MRS PLATT. I thought he might. What's he in for?

KEMP. Nerves. He had a breakdown – went berserk. Hit their foreman.

MRS PLATT. Did he.

KEMP. Working away there he was. He'd done it for years. Then all of a sudden he clouts the foreman.

MRS PLATT. I don't understand it. It makes no sense. He looks harmless enough. Still you never can tell from a man's face what he may be thinking. He may look harmless, but is he?

KEMP. Apparently not.

MRS PLATT. He often isn't. It just goes to show you can't judge by appearances. (*Rummages in bag.*) I know what I've got here for you. I clean forgot. (*Hands him snapshot.*)

KEMP. What is it?

MRS PLATT. Janice.

KEMP. She's getting a big girl.

MRS PLATT. Takes after Madge. Madge was always on the big side.

KEMP. What's this in the background?

MRS PLATT. The horse.

KEMP. The horse?

MRS PLATT. Didn't I tell you? Janice goes horseback riding now, in the country on Saturday afternoons. That's the horse she rides. Regular as clockwork.

KEMP. Where does Madge get the money from?

MRS PLATT. That's what I'd like to know. Though Fred's earning good money now. That's why she doesn't mind spending a bob or two on those lessons. The lady at the riding school has taken quite a fancy to Janice – so Madge tells me.

KEMP. Go on.

MRS PLATT. She's a smart woman. Very smart. It'll do Janice good. That kind of woman can bring a girl out.

KEMP. As long as she doesn't bring her out too far.

MRS PLATT. I don't think there's any risk of that.

KEMP. Who's that holding the horse?

MRS PLATT. That's her. The woman I was telling you of. A refined expression, hasn't she? I mean, you'd trust your daughter with her. (*Pause.*) You can't run a stables and not be otherwise.

KEMP. That's a nice dog there.

MRS PLATT. A corgi.

KEMP. I think it is.

MRS PLATT. Madge says that Janice is on about having one. She's seen this woman's dog and wants one for herself.

KEMP. That'll be the size of it.

MRS PLATT. They're all the same. What one has, the other wants. (*Pause.*) It must cost her a bit. There's the hire of the horse. Janice hasn't one of her own, you know. There's no room for a horse where they live.

Silence.

KEMP. Janice is keen on it though?

MRS PLATT. Very keen.

KEMP. Madge hasn't been in to see me.

MRS PLATT. She's busy.

KEMP. No, she doesn't care. Never did.

MRS PLATT. You don't realise how full her hands are what with Fred out all day and Janice growing so fast. (*Pause.*) Did I tell you Mrs Flackwell had brought off the treble chance?

KEMP. No.

MRS PLATT. Everyone had it last week. Twenty-eight and ninepence. Still that's not a bad return for sixpence. It isn't, is it?

KEMP. I suppose not.

MRS PLATT. Have you finished with it? (*Takes back photograph.*) I shall have to be off. I only dropped in for a few minutes.

KEMP. Will you be coming tomorrow?

MRS PLATT. I expect so. I'm not over-fond of this place. Is there anything special I can bring in when I do come?

KEMP. Some oranges.

MRS PLATT. I expect you'd like that.

KEMP. I'd appreciate an orange. Or a nice soft pear.

MRS PLATT. You've got expensive tastes! I'll look around for Jaffas then. (*Pause.*) I expect by Easter you'll be on your feet. You can sit in the park. They've painted that shelter.

KEMP. Have they?

MRS PLATT. Yes, painted it green. It'll be waiting for you.

KEMP. That's nice.

MRS PLATT. You want to hurry up and get better.

KEMP. I don't feel so bad today.

MRS PLATT. I can see that. (*Picking up her hold-all.*) I shall be off then. Cheerio. (*Giving perfunctory kiss.*)

KEMP. Ta, ta. Mind how you cross that road.

MRS PLATT. Don't you worry. I can take care of myself. Bye, bye.

She turns and goes off. He puts on his earphones, then takes them off. Sits dangling them in his hands. SIMS enters.

SIMS. I saw your visitor go.

KEMP. Yes.

SIMS. Are you comfortable?

KEMP. Thank you.

SIMS. Shall I get you a jug of water?

KEMP. No, thanks. (*Pause.*) She's coming again tomorrow.

SIMS (*going to window*). Is she?

KEMP. Yes.

SIMS. Does she have far to come?

KEMP. A fair way.

SIMS. There's a lot of people about for a Wednesday morning.
A lot of traffic.

KEMP. It's the same everywhere. (*Pause.*) I expect it'll be
better when summer comes.

SIMS. No, it gets worse with the summer.

KEMP. Don't say that!

SIMS. A lot of them lay their cars up for the winter. In summer
we have them streaming by morning, noon, and night. But
what can you do?

KEMP. It's not right.

SIMS. No.

KEMP. They ought to do something about it.

SIMS. They're going to do something, I've heard.

KEMP. What?

SIMS. I don't know.

KEMP. Bang, bang, bang. You can't get away from it. They've
no consideration.

Sound of pneumatic drill.

SIMS. They've had the road up six times already outside there.
(*Looking from window.*) There goes your daughter now. She
seems in a hurry.

KEMP. She'll have to be getting a move on to get home before the rush.

SIMS. Rushing about like that can be dangerous.

KEMP. Yes.

SIMS. We don't want to have her in here as well. Oh, watch how you go!

KEMP. What's the matter?

SIMS. There she goes – threading her way among the traffic.

KEMP. To catch her bus. That's to catch her bus.

SIMS. She's a wonderful woman, for her age. Is she your only daughter?

KEMP. Only one living. Yes.

Sound of crash, brakes squealing.

What is it?

SIMS (*starting back*). Nothing.

KEMP. What's happened?

SIMS (*pale-faced*). It's nothing. There's been an accident. You mustn't look.

KEMP. Someone's been knocked over!

SIMS. You mustn't look!

KEMP (*climbing up on his bed*). It's my daughter!

He sways, cackles hysterically, sits down suddenly. Stops laughing. SIMS stares at him. He stares at her as the scene fades out.

ACT THREE

Several days later.

A female ward. MRS PLATT *is sitting in bed. The bell goes for visiting time. Footsteps approach over polished wood floors.* MR KEMP *appears in his dressing gown.*

KEMP. Here you are then.

MRS PLATT. Oh, here you are. (*Pause.*) I didn't know whether they'd let you come round to see me.

KEMP. Yes, I was feeling much better. It's warm out. Just like spring. How are you?

MRS PLATT. A bit better.

KEMP. I was worried about you yesterday. I can tell you. Worried.

MRS PLATT. There's no need.

KEMP. Madge came in to see me. I told her what a fright you'd given me.

MRS PLATT. She never came in before.

KEMP. She wasn't allowed.

MRS PLATT (*rummaging under her pillow*). I've had a letter this morning from Mrs Flackwell.

KEMP. What does she say?

MRS PLATT. Nothing much. They're having trouble again with their Molly.

KEMP. Oh.

MRS PLATT. Yes. I don't know why she tells me these things, I'm sure. It's very embarrassing – I wish she wouldn't.

KEMP. What's the matter with Molly?

MRS PLATT. The usual. (*Sighing.*) Molly was always the
wild one. It's all on account of her being born between two
boys – she got spoiled. How many times have I said to Mrs
Flackwell: 'Evie, you'll have trouble with that girl'?

KEMP. You have.

MRS PLATT. I know, it upsets me. I think the world of Molly.
Still, it isn't the kind of thing you like to hear about. And
that Mrs Flackwell spares me no details – not one.

KEMP. Is that so?

MRS PLATT (*lowering her voice*). Apparently the police-
woman said she'd never come across a case like it. I expect
she was exaggerating though. They're great ones for
exaggerating, these policewomen. I shall tell Mrs Flackwell
so – when I see her. That's what I'll tell her. I daresay she
stands in need of a bit of comfort.

KEMP. She's got no control over Molly.

MRS PLATT. Control?

KEMP. She's not got a bit. Does just what she likes.
Absolutely.

MRS PLATT. Oh, I agree with you. Goes to school if she
feels like it, and doesn't if she doesn't. I shall tell Evie
that as well. I shall have to run the risk of offending her.
(*Cheering up.*) Though, likely as not, those policemen are
making a mountain out of a mole-hill. All the same you
do hear of some terrible things happening. It makes you
wonder. You hear so many awful things.

Pause.

A bridge collapsed on a young bride the other day,
according to the *Daily Mirror*. I ask you. Who was in
charge of it? They couldn't have been doing their job
properly or it would never have happened. And then the
very next day I read of a terrible tragedy to a bride of
eighteen. What must she feel like? It makes you wonder.
They didn't tell her at first. It'll be a shock to her when
she finds out. I hate to hear of sad things happening. They

didn't have a chance. Not a chance. They had all their lives
before them, and this has to happen. I lay awake half the
night thinking about it.

Pause.

I can't understand a girl like Molly. Her mother'll have to
take a day off work to go to the police court. She doesn't
get paid either – she'll lose money over it.

KEMP. I put the blame on her parents. She should have been
taught.

MRS PLATT. Of course she should.

KEMP. It's wrong. They ought to face up to responsibilities.

MRS PLATT. You're never going to tell me a girl of her age . .
. Well, it's too late now.

KEMP. Too late.

MRS PLATT. The damage is done. As things stand, I doubt if
it can ever be repaired. I may be getting old, but things like
this worry me. They do.

KEMP. I suppose Mrs Flackwell will be going round with a
face as long as a fiddle?

MRS PLATT. No doubt.

KEMP. Not Molly.

MRS PLATT. Not Molly. She'll be revelling in it. It might be
the very best thing if she got sent away to a home.

KEMP. It would break Evie's heart.

MRS PLATT. It would. I think their Molly in a home would
just break her heart.

KEMP. It'd finish her!

MRS PLATT. And she hasn't properly got over Stanley yet.
Some people seem fated. I wish there was something I
could do.

KEMP. Well, there isn't.

MRS PLATT. No.

KEMP. So you put your mind at rest.

MRS PLATT. I wish I could. But you know me – always
worrying. Something glandular, I expect. Of course I don't
know – I'm no authority. All the same I wouldn't be
surprised to hear that it was.

KEMP (*wriggling*). I don't think this chair is as comfortable as
the other one.

MRS PLATT. What other one?

KEMP. The one by my bed.

MRS PLATT. Oh?

KEMP. That one's more springy.

MRS PLATT. They're all the same.

KEMP. No, this one isn't so comfy. There's not enough give in
it. That one across by the window looks nice.

MRS PLATT. It's the same kind of chair.

KEMP. No.

MRS PLATT. I think it is.

KEMP. Do you think I could change them?

MRS PLATT. It's not worth it.

KEMP. If I changed them, the Sister would never notice.

MRS PLATT. You'll have to be quick. There she is.

KEMP. Would she be cross? What? I wouldn't like to be
caught in the act.

MRS PLATT. Wait until next time. Don't do it now.

KEMP. I'm not. I'm only easing my position. Are they grapes
you've got there?

MRS PLATT. Want one?

KEMP. You can eat a grape any time. (*Takes several.*)

MRS PLATT. I'm not fond of them. Much too watery. You feel cheated after a grape. I like a nice apple. What are you doing?

KEMP. I must sit on the bed. (*Doing so.*) That chair is making me feel ill.

MRS PLATT. Is it not comfortable?

KEMP. It isn't. (*Pause.*) Old Wilkins went at the weekend – did I tell you?

MRS PLATT. That nice old man in the end bed?

KEMP. Yes.

MRS PLATT. What a shame. It does seem a pity. He hadn't retired long?

KEMP. No.

MRS PLATT. It makes you wonder why such things happen. It does seem awful. He was a young man – young for nowadays, I should say.

KEMP. His family will be feeling a bit low.

MRS PLATT. They'll have to postpone the wedding now.

KEMP. No.

MRS PLATT. They're not going to? (*He shakes his head.*) Not going to postpone the – ? oh, but I do think that's wrong. It won't look right. They should show a bit of respect. No sooner get him into the grave than they're dancing about. It's downright disrespectful. If I was his granddaughter, it'd upset me. He ought to mean something to her. But that's the trouble nowadays – no respect! I know life has got to go on, but it ought not to go on so quickly.

KEMP. These young girls can't wait.

MRS PLATT. I expect that's it. I expect it's her fault. No sooner are they out of school, than they want to get married. I don't suppose she can even cook. (*Pause.*) They're supposed to leave school trained in cooking – supposed, I say! Why, they can't even boil an egg. Some of these

young girls' ideas of cooking are rudimentary. Rudimentary!
They couldn't boil a kettle. It's not right. And yet they go
and get married.

KEMP. I blame the parents.

MRS PLATT. I should say it's the parents who are to blame.
Definitely. They want to put their feet down. Mind you,
some of these young girls aren't bad. Give credit where
credit's due. Some of them have got their heads screwed on.
Our Janice says she's not going to get married until she's
twenty-one. Well, that's sensible. She'll have had time to
mature. These young girls that rush into marriage, don't
understand what's involved. They're not as innocent as
I was, but they don't know as much as they think they do.

KEMP. That's no bad thing.

MRS PLATT. No. I do think you should approach marriage
knowing something.

SISTER MARQUAND *appears.*

SISTER. Don't sit on the bed, if you don't mind.

KEMP. Don't sit on the bed?

SISTER. Sit on the chair that's provided.

KEMP. Oh, very well.

A door slams loudly.

SISTER. Listen to them! They've no consideration. Banging
the doors shut – you'd think you were in an asylum!

She disappears.

MRS PLATT. You're not supposed to sit on the bed.

KEMP. I sit on the bed in the other ward.

MRS PLATT. You're not supposed to.

KEMP. No one said anything about it in there.

MRS PLATT. Well, you know her. She looks as though she
had starch for breakfast. She's not married, is she?

KEMP. No.

MRS PLATT. I wouldn't think so. I know her type. Likes to take it out on you. Sometimes you'd wonder if they were human. I spoke to her, when I came to visit you in the other ward. Did I tell you? After they'd moved you, and I didn't know where you were. I spoke to her. 'Oh, ask one of the nurses,' she said. Why couldn't she tell me? I bet she couldn't be bothered. Couldn't be bothered to collect her thoughts and give me a civil answer. She looks a misery. There she is, rushing up and down in her starched hat – and all the time she's in a greater state of ignorance than my cat!

KEMP. They're all the same. They want to impress people.

MRS PLATT. That's it. Ask them a question, and they don't know. Too busy thinking of other things. (*Pause.*) It's the staff shortage, I expect. They have to take what they can get. Anything the Labour Exchange likes to send along. That's it, isn't it? She's taking advantage of full employ- ment. In the old days, she'd have been out of a job. I know her kind – selfishness. That's all they think about. Self, self, self. She was in a hurry just now to get off and have a chat in her office over a cup of tea. Everyone's in a hurry nowadays. Rush, rush, rush. Where's it all going to stop?

KEMP, *who has nodded off, snores slightly.*

CAMERON (*appearing over his shoulder*). He's gone to sleep.

MRS PLATT. Well, isn't that like him? They'll be ringing the bell soon, won't they?

CAMERON. Not for ten minutes. Who were you talking about?

MRS PLATT. When?

CAMERON. Just now.

MRS PLATT. Oh. Only that sister.

CAMERON. Which one?

MRS PLATT. The one in the glasses.

CAMERON. Sister Marquand.

MRS PLATT. Is that her name?

CAMERON. Here, let me make you more comfortable. (*Plumps up her pillow.*) That's better. Makes all the difference.

MRS PLATT. Thank you.

CAMERON. What's the matter with her?

MRS PLATT. Who?

CAMERON. The sister.

MRS PLATT. I don't know. It's a man, I shouldn't wonder. Women like that never give up. They never admit defeat. She'll be after some man when she's a hundred. She must be a good age now. You can tell by her mouth. Still she may have had an unhappy life. She may have adopted her attitude out of disappointment. You can't go around with a long face for ever though. You make the best of it. I thought at one time that I should never smile again.

CAMERON. But you do.

MRS PLATT. Of course you do. Is he still asleep?

CAMERON. Yes.

MRS PLATT. I don't know if he is. He can be very deaf if he wants to. (*Pause.*) Nearly all the doctors here seem to be women?

CAMERON. There are quite a few. I prefer them really.

MRS PLATT. You do?

CAMERON. The men are very tight-fisted. They wouldn't give you a smile. That Dr Barnes is a lovely woman.

MRS PLATT. Is she?

CAMERON. So kind, so gentle. And so considerate. She's the only one here that's worth anything.

MRS PLATT. Have you been a nurse long?

CAMERON. Not long.

MRS PLATT. You'll be thinking of getting married?

CAMERON. Er – yes.

MRS PLATT. Perhaps not though – it's a kind of vocation, isn't it? Like a Nun. (*Pause.*) He tells me that Mr Wilkins died. Was it expected?

CAMERON. Yes.

MRS PLATT. I expect you always expect it. They may look as right as rain to us, but you know. It doesn't come as any surprise to you, does it? You know. You know from the X-rays, the blood-tests, the temperature charts. (*Pause.*) If only he'd waited until after the wedding. It had nothing to do with him, though, did it? He had no choice.

CAMERON. What wedding would that be?

MRS PLATT. His granddaughter's. You know, the pretty one.

CAMERON. No, I never saw any of them. I only last week came onto this ward.

MRS PLATT. Then I don't suppose you would. (*Pause.*) That girl can't think much of him. Not much. You'd think she'd allow a decent period of mourning. That's the least you could expect. But no. She'll want to be off. I've been married for thirty years. That's a long time. They think that it's just one long honeymoon, but it's not. There's not much that you can tell me about marriage.

CAMERON (*yawning*). I don't suppose so.

MRS PLATT. You must be tired?

CAMERON. I am.

MRS PLATT. I expect that you'll put your feet up?

CAMERON. I will, don't worry. I'm going off duty after tea.

MRS PLATT. I feel like that sometimes. I feel as though I could sleep for a fortnight. It must be a long day for you.

CAMERON. It is.

MRS PLATT. That was what got me down on the buses. Up
and down, up and down, all day long. My feet used to burn
by the time I knocked off. Burning they were! I'd sit for
hours with them in a bowl of water. Yes, I'd have my tea
and listen to the news with my feet in a bowl. (*Pause.*) I
was just wondering . . . not that it's anything to do with me
. . . but that was an interesting thing you were saying about
that Dr Barnes. I'd never trust myself in the hands of some
of these doctors.

CAMERON. Some of them . . .

MRS PLATT. What?

Silence.

You said some of them? Were you going to say anything?

CAMERON. No.

MRS PLATT. I thought you were. (*Confidentially.*) Do you
know, I don't believe some of them are doctors at all.
They're students. Nothing but students. You never know
whether they're not just using you for an experiment.
Whether you're not their first case. It's all an experiment
really, isn't it? Sometimes it frightens me.

CAMERON (*looking away*). Excuse me –

MRS PLATT. What?

CAMERON. I thought that was Sister.

MRS PLATT. No. Do you know, I lie awake at night
sometimes and think what would happen if they put a
student onto me. Oh, you can laugh, nurse, but it's a real
fear!

CAMERON. I wouldn't laugh.

MRS PLATT. I should be very surprised if you did. You don't
look the kind of girl that'd laugh when somebody told you
their secret fears. All the same, I don't believe some of
these hospitals care. What is it to them? It might be your
father or your mother lying in that bed, but to them it's just
hard work. (*Pause.*) I don't believe some of these students

are hardly trained at all. It's a shocking waste of affairs, but what can you do? It's a shocking waste of time. You might as well save your breath. I've no doubt, nurse, just by looking at one of these students, you can tell whether he's in control. You can tell at a glance. But I can't. No. It isn't possible. I haven't got the qualifications.

Pause.

I always blame our own doctor for Mum's death. She was only seventy-four. I don't care who hears it. He caused her death by neglect.

CAMERON. Don't excite yourself!

MRS PLATT. What did you say?

CAMERON. You know what the doctor said.

MRS PLATT. Well, you are in a depressing mood. I suppose she'll be in in a minute with that bell of hers. What with that and the crows' feet round her eyes, it makes her an object of terror. She handles it like a club! The way she stands there waving it, you'd wonder if she was qualified to care for the sick.

CAMERON. I must go now.

MRS PLATT (*dispiritedly*). Oh, very well. (*Nudges* KEMP.)

KEMP. What is it?

MRS PLATT. I've woken you.

KEMP. I wish you wouldn't.

We follow CAMERON *into the nurses' room.*

BROWN (*pointedly*). She looks very drawn.

CAMERON. Oh, shut up.

SIMS (*still knitting*). She works too hard, poor dear. I'm sure she overdoes it.

BROWN. Go on.

CAMERON. Have you done?

BROWN. Look at her eyes, quite violet those bags.

SIMS. The strain shows.

CAMERON. Have you finished?

SIMS. When do you go off duty?

CAMERON. After tea.

BROWN. Say what you like, she's a trouper!

SIMS. Where have you been?

CAMERON. That Mrs Platt caught me.

SIMS. Poor you!

BROWN. She'd talk the hind leg off a donkey, that woman.

CAMERON. Ever since they put Sister Marquand on this ward, it's been like Bedlam. She's even getting on the visitors' nerves.

Enter FAZAKERLEY.

FAZAKERLEY. Is there a cup of tea left for me? (*She sits down and opens her book.*)

SIMS (*pouring one*). Kemp still using the catheter?

CAMERON. Yes.

Pause.

BROWN (*to* CAMERON). Are you upset?

CAMERON. A bit.

BROWN. What's the matter?

CAMERON. It's suddenly come to me what it means.

BROWN. When did this happen?

CAMERON. Last night. All of a sudden it hit me between the eyes.

BROWN (*smugly*). I've known for a long time.

SIMS. You read between the lines too much.

BROWN. But then there are *so* many lines to read between.

CAMERON (*sniffing*). That it should happen to me of all people. It's not as if I'm promiscuous.

BROWN. No, dear.

CAMERON. I keep myself to myself.

SIMS. Of course you do.

BROWN. She's right. She's told me many a time how much self-control she has. Haven't you, dear?

SIMS. Shut up.

BROWN. Time and again.

CAMERON (*suddenly*). I shall have to get married.

BROWN. What for?

CAMERON. The baby.

BROWN. D'you think it'll mind?

CAMERON. I know what these society tarts do, but I wouldn't dream of it. I must get married.

SIMS. Will he?

CAMERON. He's asked me often enough.

BROWN. No problem then.

CAMERON. There is. I don't know whether I love him.

BROWN. Hark at her!

SIMS. I give up.

BROWN. What were you doing to lose control in the first place?

   CAMERON *starts to cry.*

FAZAKERLEY. Do you mind? I'm trying to read.

BROWN. It's a nice time now to start wondering.

CAMERON. I wish I could make up my mind.

BROWN. You mustn't make a habit of it.

CAMERON. I could never marry a man I don't love. And then living in married quarters . . .

SIMS. What married quarters?

CAMERON. He's in the army.

SIMS. Eileen!

BROWN. You must be off your flipping head.

CAMERON. Why?

BROWN. Going round with that type.

CAMERON. He's got nice eyes.

BROWN. Are they his own?

SIMS. They make a habit of it, they do. *And* they don't take precautions.

BROWN. It was the uniform that got you – no need to tell me! You had to have something fancy – and it's all because she's frigid. No, but you are. You told me.

SIMS. Without his uniform, she wouldn't look at him.

BROWN. *Wouldn't* she? You don't know Eileen. How old is he?

CAMERON. Eighteen.

BROWN. You want your head examining, love! They'll have you for kidnapping. (*Pause.*) Well, never mind. Least said, soonest mended. Sims here can knit you a layette.

SIMS. I will if you like?

CAMERON. Would you?

SIMS. You buy the wool.

BROWN. But you'd better watch out. Look at that! A cardigan she's calling it. She'll make your baby clothes to fit an elephant. Look at her – got the wrong needles, cast on too many stitches, and look at the colour – enough to blind a bat. (*Critically.*) I suppose you might use it to camouflage a pillar-box.

SIMS (*apologetically*). It's for my Mum.

BROWN. She must have a figure.

SIMS. She's got a 34 inch bust and 52 inch hips. What can you wear on that, I ask you?

BROWN. Ever thought of a tent?

O'HARA *comes into the door with a trolley.*

SIMS. It is difficult.

BROWN. Has she ever thought of slimming?

SIMS. It doesn't agree with her. It made her feel bad.

BROWN. It'd make me feel bad to have to look at her. She must be a sight. No offence meant.

O'HARA *pushes the trolley off at other door.*

How is it you're so small?

SIMS. I take after Dad.

FAZAKERLEY *rises.*

BROWN. Oh, it's alive!

FAZAKERLEY. Did you say anything, Brown?

BROWN. Listen! It can speak. No, to tell you the truth, dear, I was worried. I thought you'd passed out. I thought you'd gone into a trance. It's this reading. She overdoes it.

FAZAKERLEY *shrugs and exits.*

A facey devil, she is.

SIMS. She's quiet.

BROWN. She's not bad. I have her on, I do. I have a good laugh. That book she's reading – it makes me die. You didn't really think it was about swans, did you?

O'HARA (*returning*). What is it about?

BROWN. Listen to her! Alice O'Hara, the idiot's friend. It's by Proust, you nit.

O'HARA. She must be very intelligent.

BROWN. Some of the things she tells me – that Proust is full of smut.

SIMS. No!

O'HARA. Are you sure?

BROWN. Unless she makes it all up. But she couldn't – it's too good.

O'HARA. These books shouldn't be allowed.

BROWN. They're crude. Very crude.

O'HARA. No wonder that everybody's going on the streets.

BROWN. You speak for yourself!

O'HARA. I can't understand people writing that kind of book.

SIMS. Can't you?

O'HARA. What kind of mind must they have?

BROWN. Depraved. But the way that he puts it is most entertaining.

O'HARA. I wouldn't be entertained.

BROWN. You wouldn't be entertained by anything except the Catholic Ladies' fun book.

SIMS. This Proust, he must have been hot.

O'HARA. Daniel Proust. I think I've heard of him.

BROWN. He's French, you nit. You'll be making out he's Daniel O'Proust in a minute. You Paddies are all the same.

O'HARA. I thought it was Daniel. What was it?

BROWN. André. André Proust from Montmartre. You want to ask her to read you a bit. It'd make your hair curl.

SIMS. Seriously?

BROWN. You ask Fazakerley.

O'HARA. I'll take your word.

Enter SISTER. *They stand.*

SISTER. Which of you is supposed to be on duty?

O'HARA (*quickly*). I've just come off.

SISTER Who's on the ward now?

SIMS (*packing up her knitting*). I'm just going on.

SISTER. What's the time?

SIMS. Twenty-five past.

SISTER. What are you doing, Brown?

BROWN. I'm off duty.

SISTER. Not till four-thirty?

BROWN. No.

SISTER. It isn't four-thirty.

BROWN. No.

SISTER. What's your excuse?

BROWN. I was replacing a bottle.

SISTER. I see. You shouldn't have left the ward unattended, O'Hara.

O'HARA. Fazakerley is on duty.

SISTER. I didn't see her as I came through. Was Mr Basset given his sedative?

O'HARA. Yes, Sister.

SISTER. Did he make any objection?

O'HARA. No.

SISTER. Good.

Exit SISTER.

BROWN. I wish someone would put her up the spout!

CAMERON. That'll be the day.

BROWN. Wouldn't I laugh? I'd laugh, I would! I'd give five years of my life to see that happen. Can't you see the headlines: 'SURPRISE FOR WOMAN OF FIFTY.' 'Unattractive sister Marquand said, I had almost given up hope.'

O'HARA. It would have to be an Immaculate Conception. No man would touch her.

SIMS. She's crackers on that chap in the dispensary.

BROWN. Don't talk wet!

SIMS. She is, you know.

BROWN. Since when?

SIMS. Since she first saw him. She couldn't keep still, and her colour came and went.

BROWN. What an experience. I wonder he wasn't put off his food.

SIMS. True as I stand here.

O'HARA. I don't believe it.

SIMS. Suit yourself.

Re-enter SISTER. SIMS *makes herself scarce.* BROWN *is about to follow.*

SISTER. One moment, Brown.

BROWN. Sister?

SISTER. Mr Kemp says that he missed his supper last night?

BROWN. He was asleep.

SISTER. You should have woken him. He shouldn't go too long between meals.

BROWN. That's how ulcers start, isn't it?

SISTER. Don't ask me questions, Brown. So he had no supper? (*Pause.*) Didn't he want any?

BROWN. I daresay he wanted some. Yes.

SISTER. Why wasn't he given any?

BROWN. It was too late.

SISTER. Who told you that it was too late?

BROWN. I looked at the clock.

SISTER (*breathing heavily*). I see.

BROWN. He'd made a good tea.

SISTER. That has nothing to do with it.

BROWN. He didn't ask me for any.

SISTER. That isn't the point. (*Pause.*) Very well. I shall remember this.

Exit.

BROWN. The way she creeps about! You've got to hand it to her. Got any fags, Eileen?

CAMERON. You had my last.

SIMS *offers a packet to* BROWN.

BROWN. Got a match?

SIMS. Would you like me to smoke it for you?

FAZAKERLEY (*re-entering*). Did you see misery?

BROWN. She passed through.

FAZAKERLEY. I suppose she wondered where I was?

BROWN. She said nothing. You'll have to invite her to the wedding, Eileen. Imagine her capering about with a skinful!

O'HARA. Who's getting married?

BROWN. She is.

O'HARA. Are you?

CAMERON. I don't know.

BROWN. She just can't make up her mind.

SISTER (*re-appearing*). You'd better get into the ward, Fazakerley. I shall be ringing the bell in a few minutes.

They all busy themselves. We follow FAZAKERLEY *into the ward.*

SIMS (*as they go*). She missed you then?

FAZAKERLEY. What?

SIMS. I said she missed you. What did you do to deserve it?

Dissolve onto MRS PLATT.

KEMP. What did you say?

MRS PLATT. I could see you were miles away. While I was speaking, I said to myself: 'He's not listening.'

KEMP. I feel tired.

MRS PLATT. That's a good sign. (*Speaking loudly.*) I said that we have to go sometime.

KEMP. Go where?

MRS PLATT (*listlessly*). I don't know. We hope that it's heaven.

KEMP. You mean die?

MRS PLATT. I've never believed that death was the end.
I believe we shall see the people we love again. I was taught that we shall. I can't stand these people who try to depress you by saying there's nothing else. I always turn a deaf ear to those kind of people. How can they know? There's a woman in our street who's such an atheist. 'I'M an ATHEIST,' she'll say, as bold as brass. Miserable she is. Miserable as sin. Well, you can't put up with them, can you? You'll never get me to believe we shan't meet the people we love again. It wouldn't be natural.

KEMP. You're in a funny mood. I came in here to cheer you up.

MRS PLATT. I wonder if it'll be just like going to sleep.

KEMP. It frightens me when you talk like that.

MRS PLATT. Going to sleep is nice.

KEMP (*nodding off*). Very nice.

MRS PLATT. Of course it is. I remember when Eddie went . . .
Funny. I can't remember what he looked like now. We had
a snap of him taken in the back garden when he was a kid.
That's how I remember him. I never thought I'd forget
Eddie's face. But I did. He'd have been almost forty if he'd
been alive. He'd have been married, with kids of his own.
How time flies. It's doesn't seem long, though. It doesn't
seem long.

FAZAKERLEY. Are you all right?

MRS PLATT. Yes.

FAZAKERLEY. You don't want anything?

MRS PLATT. No, thank you.

FAZAKERLEY (*looking at* MR KEMP). He's gone to sleep
again.

MRS PLATT. I don't know how he can. Not in the chair like
that! (*Pause.*) He's getting better, you know, but he won't
admit it.

FAZAKERLEY. No?

MRS PLATT. He doesn't like to admit it. Thinks he may not
get quite so much sympathy when he's better.

FAZAKERLEY. You're right there.

MRS PLATT. I bet he's not really asleep. He pretends he can't
hear us, but he can. Look at him lying there – there's a
smile on his face.

FAZAKERLEY *goes round the bed to look at him.*

He's a bit of an old beggar!

FAZAKERLEY. Don't tease him. He looks –

MRS PLATT. What is it?

FAZAKERLEY. I wouldn't have had this happen for all the
world –

Dissolve to the nurses' room.

O'HARA. I had five bob on each way.

BROWN. You're mad. Her tips will ruin you, girl. What's it like out?

O'HARA. All right.

BROWN. Come on then, for Christ's sake. I want to get out of this dump. I'm not stopping here all night. Are you coming?

O'HARA. Yes.

FAZAKERLEY runs in.

BROWN. What's all the rush about?

FAZAKERLEY. It's number three – he's passed out! She's playing merry hell in there. You can say you were washing up. Quick!

SIMS rushes out. General confusion. Dissolve to MRS PLATT saying:

MRS PLATT. He's . . . dead.

The bell goes for the end of visiting time.

Fade out.